MATURE STUDENTS' DIRECTORY 2004

Lifelong learning opportunities for the 21-plus

3rd edition

Margaret Flynn

The Mature Students' Directory 2004
This third edition published in 2004 by Trotman and Company Ltd
2 The Green
Richmond
Surrey TW9 1PL
Formerly published as *The Mature Students' Guide*

Editorial and Publishing Team
Author Margaret Flynn
Editorial Mina Patria, Editorial Director; Rachel Lockhart, Commissioning Editor; Anya Wilson, Editor; Erin Milliken, Editorial Assistant
Production Ken Ruskin, Head of Pre-press and Production
Sales and Marketing Deborah Jones, Head of Sales and Marketing

Designed by Ursula McLaughlin

British Library Cataloguing in Publication Data
A catalogue record for this book is available from the British Library

ISBN 0 85660 888 2

Typeset by Mac Style Ltd, Scarborough, N. Yorkshire
Printed and bound in Great Britain by Creative Print & Design (Wales) Ltd

CONTENTS

INTRODUCTION

Steady increases in the number of mature students entering higher education have positive results for all involved:

- adults returning to study hope this will benefit them in terms of their personal lives and career ambitions
- colleges and universities are enriched by a diverse student population
- successive governments have encouraged widening participation in education, leading to a better skilled workforce.

The number of older students in each institution varies, from just a few to over half. Nationally, in 2002, 23 per cent of all those accepted on to full-time higher education courses were mature students.

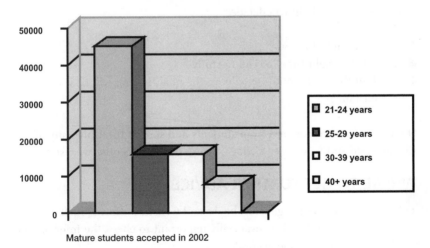

Mature students accepted in 2002

(Source: UCAS Data and Analytical Services and HESA)

The number of mature students on part-time courses is much higher – over 60 per cent in 2001. (Source: www.agr.org.uk/news)

WHO IS A MATURE STUDENT?

Anyone who enters a course in further or higher education aged over 21 is considered to be a mature student.

All mature students have different circumstances and background experiences. As a result, every application from a mature student for a higher education course is considered on its own merits, and entry requirements for mature students will vary at different higher education institutions.

PURPOSE OF THIS DIRECTORY

This directory is aimed at adults unfamiliar with the higher education system in the UK and who want to enter it for the first time. If you have some knowledge of the system you may find it useful to update yourself on recent changes, especially with student funding. Further education courses are mentioned as a means of getting into a higher level course – but are not covered in any detail.

This directory can help you decide:

- if study is right for you
- if this is the right time for you to study
- which of the many routes to achieve the qualification will fit with your circumstances.

Quotes in this directory are from students and staff at the University of Birmingham and University College, Worcester, unless otherwise stated.

WHERE TO GET FURTHER ADVICE

This directory refers to agencies, books and websites offering further advice and information. It is especially important to check the information you have is up to date and accurate.

Try to ensure any advice and guidance you get is impartial. If that is not possible, obtain several points of view before making a decision that could so drastically affect your life.

You could try:

- Information, Advice and Guidance (IAG) worker
- course tutor – for A-level or Access courses
- university pre-entry guidance worker
- admissions staff in universities and colleges of higher education
- Connexions or careers adviser
- books, e.g. *How to Complete your UCAS Form* (Trotman).

'*If they want to talk it over with someone, there'll always be an IAG network in every area and the best way to find out about this is to go to their local Connexions office or there may be IAG workers at a local FE college. Alternatively, they could find out about local IAGs from the LSC (Learning and Skills Council). If you are at a college already, there will be a career adviser and your course tutor who can help. There may also be a pre-entry guidance worker at the local university. Some Connexions services may see adults, but there may be restrictions on who you can see.*'
Rose Watson, Pre-entry advice and guidance worker.

Careers services work mainly with under-19-year-olds and are called Connexions Service (in England), Careers Scotland, Careers Wales and Northern Ireland Careers Service.

Much advice and guidance is provided free, but in some cases you would need to pay. For example, the Birmingham and Solihull Connexions service charges employed adults. They provide a range of services, such as a half-hour interview for £30.

The Guidance Council (www.guidancecouncil.com) and Learning and Skills Council (www.lsc.gov.uk) provide links to information about local guidance provision. Public libraries may be able to provide contact details for local advice or have a copy of the *Directory of Guidance Provision for Adults in the UK* (ADSET) you could consult.

CHAPTER ONE

WHAT'S ON OFFER?

> ## Key Points
>
> - The majority of adults entering higher education do a first degree course, but there are alternatives you could consider before making a decision.
> - Modular courses are now very widespread.
> - Many courses can be studied in different ways – full-time, part-time, by distance learning, e-learning or learning through work schemes.

As a mature student, you have a wide range of options open to you in terms of how and what you can study if you are considering a higher education course. This chapter defines the main options so that you can make a more informed choice about the next step.

A starting point is to define the distinction between further and higher education.

Further education (FE) is provided mainly through local further education or technical colleges; a wide variety of academic, vocational and leisure-oriented courses is taught both to school leavers and older students. Many of the courses available at FE colleges (such as A-levels, BTECs and GCSEs) are entrance qualifications for higher education. There are other special courses, known as access courses, for mature students with few formal educational qualifications who want to enter higher education.

Higher education (HE) is provided largely through universities and colleges of HE. These offer degree, diploma, certificate and professional courses in a wide variety of subjects. The majority of their students will study on three-year degree programmes. The standard entry requirement for these courses is A-levels or their equivalent but alternative entrance procedures exist for those who are over 21 years of age when they start their studies.

The distinction is becoming blurred, as it is now possible to do at least part of a degree course at FE colleges, and universities are offering more sub-degree-level work.

HIGHER EDUCATION AWARDS

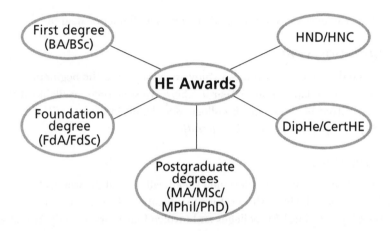

First degrees

The majority of students in HE are studying first degree courses and are known as undergraduates. Of those full-time mature students who accepted places in 2002, 88 per cent were on degree courses. Most full-time degree courses last for three years and when successfully completed, you are awarded a 'Bachelor's' degree by the university. Most courses are awarded at 'honours' level, but there are some degrees that are classed as 'ordinary' as they involve slightly less complex study. The most common degree titles are:

- BA – Bachelor of Arts
- BSc – Bachelor of Science
- BEng – Bachelor of Engineering

Some first degree courses last longer than three years, particularly those related to specific professional training, such as architecture or medicine. Many other degrees include a 'year out', working in an occupation related to the degree subject (e.g. engineering) and are referred to as 'sandwich courses'. Language degrees usually involve a year abroad.

Once you have completed the course, you will be awarded a level of achievement. The classifications for honours degrees are: First; Upper Second (2:1); Lower Second (2:2); Third; Pass; Fail.

The Pass category does not normally count as an 'honours' degree.

Foundation years

For some degree courses you can study an extra year at the beginning, known as a foundation year or Year 0. These are sometimes available at the university itself or run at an FE college. See details in Chapter Five *Getting In – qualifications and preparation.*

2+2 degrees

These full-time courses are designed specifically for adults who lack formal qualifications and who wish to return to education. They are run in partnership with local FE colleges and involve four years of study: two at a local college and two taking standard university courses alongside other students.

Foundation degrees

Foundation degrees (FdA or FdSc) last for two years if studied full-time and combine academic theory and practical work in subjects such as health care, early childhood, e-commerce and digital business. In some cases, students can then progress onto the third year of a BA/BSc degree course. These degrees have been on offer since 2001 and are validated by the Foundation Degree Forward. One feature is that employers play a significant role in designing the courses, meaning key skills necessary in the workplace are included. There are now about 12,000 students on foundation degrees. Further information can be found on the website: www.foundationdegree.org.uk.

Higher National Diplomas (HND) and Higher National Certificates (HNC)

A full-time HND course lasts for two years but can also be studied part-time.

HND and HNC courses are taught in universities, colleges of HE and some colleges of FE. Subjects cover a wide range and include: business studies, graphic design, information technology, leisure studies, media production and social care.

The HND qualification is fully recognised in its own right by employers, but after successfully completing an HND it is possible (with some exceptions) to transfer to a degree course. You can enter the final year of a closely related degree programme, gain direct entry into the second year of a related degree programme, or use your HND as an entry qualification into the first year of a completely unrelated degree.

Diploma of Higher Education (DipHE)

Diplomas of HE require two years of full-time study. With a further year's study you can top up to a degree. Some professional areas, such as youth, play and community work or nursing, tend to lead to diplomas of HE. Some students who just complete part of a degree course are awarded a Diploma of HE for two years' study or a Certificate of HE for one year.

Postgraduate higher degrees and diplomas

There are also 'higher' or Master's degrees (e.g. MA, MSc, MPhil) and doctorates (PhD) that can follow on from first degrees and place more emphasis on individual research. You often need to have achieved a 2:1 classification in your first degree to get a place on a higher degree course.

WHAT SUBJECTS CAN YOU STUDY?

Students studying a degree course can choose to study:

- a single subject area or discipline
- two subjects equally (a joint course)

■ a major/minor course (when you study one subject more than the other)
■ a general combined studies course with a wide choice of modules.

Some of these are similar to the subjects studied at school, such as history, English literature and maths, but many other subjects less common in schools, such as environmental science and women's studies, are taught in HE. Some courses are related directly to a career, such as nursing or physiotherapy, giving qualifications necessary to getting a job. Others are 'non-vocational' and have less direct links to a specific career area.

Modular courses

Students follow a programme of study that consists of a fixed number of separate courses (or 'modules' in many institutions). You can usually choose a number of modules, but some courses may be compulsory, particularly at the outset of the programme. Modules are at different levels – 1, 2 and 3. You would usually need to study a module at level 1 before progressing on to level 2 in the same subject area.

Each module is assigned a number of credits and for an honours degree, you would need to gain 360 credits, for a foundation degree 240, etc.

To see the range of courses available, look at the UCAS website (www.ucas.com), which lists over 50,000 courses.

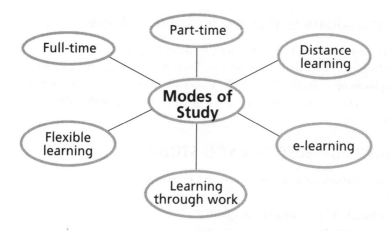

MODES OF STUDY

In the past, studying full-time (where you attended a university or college) was the only option. This is no longer the case. There are now new methods of study, which means you can study more flexibly (part- or full-time) – perhaps through distance learning, e-learning or work-based learning. You can study the first year (or possibly year 2) in a local FE college before attending the university to complete the degree course. (See details on foundation years and 2+2 courses, page 6.)

All of these developments mean there is a greater chance of finding a course that allows you to study in a way that suits your particular circumstances and preferences.

Universities and colleges usually run courses over an academic year (September to June), divided into three terms or two semesters.

Full-time study at a college/university

'I have eight contact hours a week although it has gone down to six this semester because I'm doing a dissertation. The rest of the time is spent on independent study – reading and working on my own.'
Jacci Qualters, English and Literary Studies and
Media and Cultural Studies student

In some subject areas, such as engineering, contact time is nearer 15 or 16 hours a week. Courses such as medicine have very full timetables, with students working 9–5 most days.

If you have restrictions on which hours you are able to attend a course, be aware that the timetable for each semester could change, depending on which modules you do. Some universities operate a 9am–9pm timetable – your module choice could be restricted if you aren't able to attend at certain times of the day/week. For details, see the university listings in this directory.

'Students should try to find out the timetable in advance – some universities are not good at this and give out timetables a week or so in advance – difficult if you have work or childcare to sort out. Even then,

at the end of a semester it changes. Students end up doing modules they didn't want to do originally because of when the lectures are.'

Rose Watson, Pre-entry guidance worker

Part-time study at a college/university

Many institutions offer a range of HE courses part-time. Some courses are designed as evening only courses, for others you attend a reduced proportion of daytime classes. On some courses, you can change the mode of study as you go along, for example, start full-time, then drop down to part-time.

'When I started, I did the first two years full-time but transport was difficult from where I lived in Herefordshire – the last bus was at 5.30pm! I decided to go part-time to help even though it meant I could only get a £500 means-tested student loan per year. I sold up in the end and moved to Worcester – a wise but drastic step.'

Penny, English and Literary Studies student

Distance learning

Degree and other HE courses are available through distance learning, where you study from home and are sent the course materials over the internet, by post in paper form, video or CD-ROM. This is sometimes called a home-study or correspondence course. Tutorial and study courses enable you to meet other students on occasions, but the bulk of the work is done on your own, with the support of a tutor.

The Open University (OU) was set up specifically for adult learners in 1969, and offers degrees and other courses by distance learning to over 190,000 students. Most courses start in February, but some in May, August and November. You can apply any time during the previous year but early application is recommended.

With the OU, you need to study courses to the value of 360 points to complete an honours degree and most students study for 60 points per year. Courses are assessed by a number of written assignments and some courses have a final exam. Further details are on the website (www.open.ac.uk).

'I was at home with two small children and it was something I could do for myself ... from home. It took me six years to complete and it built up my confidence – the more I found I could do, the more I wanted to do. When I got my degree, I really missed studying.'

Patti Rookes, OU graduate and now Wyre Forest
Lifelong Learning Networks Support Officer

Other universities and colleges provide opportunities for students to study some of their courses 'at a distance'. For details on the wide range of distance learning courses, consult these websites: www.distance-learning.hobsons.com and www.homestudy.org.uk.

Flexible learning courses

Flexible learning courses offer a number of options that are negotiated between staff and students e.g. assessment deadlines, methods of assessment.

Flexible learning can apply to distance learning, full-time and part-time courses at some institutions and encourages people to study in a way that suits them. For details, see the university listings in this directory.

Learning through work

If you want to study for a university qualification without taking time off work, there is a new scheme called 'Learning through work'. Through Learndirect (set up by UFI – University for Industry) some universities (e.g. Derby) offer a range of recognised HE qualifications. You study at your own pace, usually at work, on modules agreed with your employer, using an interactive website for tutor support. More information is on www.learndirect-ltw.co.uk.

e-learning

e-learning courses are conducted entirely via the Internet. Support from a tutor is via email, online conferences and telephone. The Open University offers courses entirely online and a new development is that some conventional universities are setting up 'virtual universities' to offer courses and resources online.

Further information on courses and subjects on offer in HE can be found on the website www.hero.ac.uk.

CHAPTER TWO

WHAT TO EXPECT

Key Points

■ Mature students find that methods of study and assessment in HE are different to what they have previously experienced.
■ Help with essential study skills is available at universities, but gaining some IT skills before you go will make your life a lot easier.
■ Mixing in with younger students is often much easier than mature students anticipate.

Now you have investigated the range of options available in HE, what else do you need to consider? This chapter gives a flavour of what to expect from university study and asks:

? How will you be asked to study?
What study facilities are there?
What help is there with study skills?
What will the other students be like?

ACADEMIC STUDY

How do students learn?

'I found the study different from what I expected – it helped that I had an interest in English and had done some creative writing courses in the past. The shift from practical to theory on a degree is the big one – sometimes it feels like several months since I picked up a paint brush. I thought that on the degree I would be taught to paint and draw to a higher standard. What happens is the tutor introduces you to the intellectual challenge of the theoretical side of studying art.'

Steve Noake, Art and Design student

In HE you will find that the way you are taught is very different to the way you were taught in school. The method of teaching and learning will vary with the subject, but the most common methods are:

■ *Lectures* – a tutor/lecturer talks to a large group (anything from 15 to 300 plus), usually for around an hour.
■ *Seminars* – small groups of students (usually no more than 20) discuss a topic under the supervision of a tutor.
■ *Tutorials* – you will be allocated a tutor with whom you can discuss work individually or in small groups. You may also be allocated a personal tutor or supervisor who can advise on other issues.
■ *Practical, or 'hands-on' work* – on some courses, such as teaching, art and science subjects, direct experience has always been an essential ingredient. In recent years this approach has been adopted increasingly in other disciplines e.g. social science students working in the community or developing questionnaires to distribute around the campus.
■ *Small group work* – one of the most valuable and accessible learning resources at your disposal is other students. Groups may work on assessed projects where research and conclusions are fed back to the bigger group via a presentation.
■ *Independent study* – as a student you will spend large amounts of time reading and absorbing what you have read, reflecting on it and writing about it. To become an effective 'independent learner' you will need to develop a range of study skills.

Study skills

In the past it was assumed that all students came into HE already equipped with the skills necessary for study, such as essay writing, notetaking and using libraries. More recently, institutions have recognised the need to provide 'study skills' help for students:

■ *Study skills courses* – examples include IT courses, and research techniques available at most universities.
■ *University websites* – some universities produce information on study skills on their website. For example, the Learner's Guide on the Open University website (www.open.ac.uk).
■ *National websites* – e.g. www.studentUK.com and www.skills4study.com have sections on academic advice.

■ *Universities' written materials* – some universities produce written materials, such as 'Moving On' – a package of information and workshop materials addressing skills for HE produced by a collaborative project between the universities of Coventry, Warwick, and University College Worcester. 'Moving On' is also on the Coventry University website (www.coventry.ac.uk – search in 'widening participation').

■ *Books* – many books are available such as:
  The Study Skills Handbook, S Cottrell (Palgrave 1999)
  The Students' Guide to Writing Essays, D. Roberts (Kogan Page 1999)

IT skills

IT skills are now essential for all students. All you need at the start is a basic ability to use the Internet and Microsoft programmes, such as Word.

'It is very important these days that students arrive at university or college as IT literate as possible. It is no longer just a recommendation – it is essential because all communications happen via the Internet and email. Some mature students take all kinds of strategies to avoid having to use IT and so don't pick up important information, or can't do fundamental things like making module choices – increasingly, there is no other way of doing it. Introduction to IT courses at university are often not basic enough and won't tell you how to turn the computer on.'
Dr Jill Terry, English Lecturer

'I did use computers at work, but we used specialist financial programmes and I wasn't familiar with the usual packages, such as Excel, Access or Word and the Windows system. Before I came, I did a few modules of the ECDL (European Computer Driving Licence), which helped.'
Steve Noake, Art and Design student

HOW ARE STUDENTS ASSESSED?

■ **Exams** – many people who did not do well at school are put off re-entering education because of their fear of exams. Exams do still play the most important part in the assessment process of many courses, but the emphasis placed on them is lessening gradually. Many institutions provide practical and moral support for those students who require it.

(Many younger students are only too grateful to receive this help as well!)

■ **Continuous assessment** – continuous assessment is where work produced is graded and used instead of, or in conjunction with, exams. As well as allowing students to work in the way that suits them best, continuous assessment also provides students with valuable feedback on how they are doing.

'My main worry was wondering if what I was writing matched with what they were expecting. Once I got over the first few weeks I found study came more easily – getting feedback from the first assignments helped.'

Kevin Boreham, Business Management student

Types of assessment

■ **Essays and coursework** – students are expected to produce written work on a regular basis for assessment.
■ **Presentations** – many modules now include either individual or group presentations of material.
■ **Dissertations** – a feature of coursework that frequently appeals to older students is a 'dissertation' or independent study project. Students are encouraged to undertake a lengthy piece of work, usually on a subject of their choosing.
■ **Practical assessments** – on some courses, especially more vocational ones e.g. teacher training, students are assessed by observers while they are on placement.

WHAT WILL THE OTHER STUDENTS BE LIKE?

Some people have preconceived ideas on this subject:

'I just thought A-level students got to go there [to college or university], that you've got to be middle class, that you must not have an accent, that you must have A-levels, you must have gone to grammar school and that was it otherwise you don't even think of applying.'

'My perception is that things are changing, but at some levels and at some institutions things have perhaps taken longer to change than others.'

(Comments from *Student Voice* – a project run by six universities in London – City, East London, London Guildhall, North London, Open University and Queen Mary, 2002.)

Things are changing in HE. In many institutions mature students account for at least a quarter of all students, and in some places more than half.

'I have friends across the age range. I find the younger students have become good friends. I have spent quite a bit of this last year being a listening ear – somebody you can talk to who is not part of the system – we all do this for each other fairly naturally.'
Penny, English and Literary Studies student

'As a mature student I did at times feel isolated – sometimes taken for granted, but then maybe I should have tried harder to join in conversations about the latest mobile phone designs or Internet chat lines. Maybe I'm jaundiced, but that's what seemed to dominate the conversation of the teenage students who, on my course, were very much in the majority.'
(The Mature Students' Guide to Higher Education 2003, UCAS, page 17)

'On my course there are very few mature students, about ten at a guess, but this hasn't been a problem. The younger students were surprised to see older people on the course, but once they realised we weren't there to make up the numbers, or that we hadn't got in through the back door, they accepted us easily. I am careful not to treat them like my children and offer unwanted advice.'
Julie Turley, Law student

Look at Chapter Eight: *When you get there* for more ideas on what to expect.

CHAPTER THREE

ISSUES TO CONSIDER

Key Points

■ For most mature students finance is a key issue and needs careful planning in great detail: fees, loans, grants, accommodation and childcare costs. Buy yourself a calculator!

■ The government is perpetually reviewing student finance. All the planned changes outlined in this chapter are subject to confirmation. Always check for the most up-to-date information with the DfES (Department for Education and Skills) or your local education authority (LEA).

■ You will need to consider the effect your new status as a 'student' will have on your personal life.

This chapter gives a basic overview of financial issues, accommodation and childcare relevant to mature students.

FINANCIAL ISSUES

Finance is a concern for students of all ages. Some mature students re-enter education with significant financial commitments, and making ends meet can become a major problem. Many students have to take paid work in order to maintain an acceptable income during their studies.

'My advice is to go direct to your LEA or DfES for information about what financial help you are eligible for. At the moment there are huge changes in the system of grants and loans for mature students, especially if you have dependants. Some information from other sources may be dated as things are moving so fast.'

Nahid Saiyed, Mature Students Co-ordinator,
Student Support and Counselling

This section will give you a basic idea how the system works, which may help you decide if HE is feasible for you.

HOW IT WORKS

There are two main costs for HE students:

- tuition fees
- living expenses.

Proposals for a review of student finance are currently under discussion, which could bring major changes for those starting a course in 2006 and some changes for 2004. Some of the student support grants are being simplified in 2003. Check the latest situation with:

- the Department for Education and Skills website: www.dfes.gov.uk/studentsupport
- DfES helpline on 0800 731 9133 or on textphone 0800 328 8988
- DfES booklets: *Financial Support for Higher Education Students; Bridging the Gap – A Guide to the Disabled Students Allowances; Childcare Grant and other Financial Help for Student Parents.* All three are available from the DfES website (under forms and guides) or in paper form from your LEA
- the local education authority (LEA) where your home is. The LEA is part of your local council – you can find the address in the business numbers section of the phone book.

The information in this section applies to students whose homes are in England and Wales. If you are a student in Scotland, you should contact the Student Awards Agency for Scotland (SAAS) for information. For Northern Ireland, you should contact the Student Support Branch of the Department for Employment and Learning (Northern Ireland).

Funding help is dependent on:

- the HE course being a 'designated course', and usually, but not always, at a university or college of HE/FE rather than a private or independent college. The DfES website details which courses are designated

■ your personal eligibility e.g. where you live/whether you have been to university before/your age.

Part-time students usually need to be studying at least 50 per cent of the equivalent full-time course to be eligible for help with funding.

Tuition fees

Since 1998, students have contributed towards the cost of tuition for their course. For 2003/4, this is a maximum of £1,125, payable each year. About half of all students do not pay this much as it is means tested. The full cost of HE courses ranges from £4,000 to £20,000 per year so it is essential that you apply to your LEA for assessment of fee contributions, or you could be eligible to pay full fees.

The level of student contribution to tuition fees is currently under review – it is proposed to allow universities to charge up to £3,000 per year, payable after completion of the course.

Full-time students

Many mature students do not pay tuition fees as they are assessed for contributions to fees as an 'independent student'. You are classed as independent if:

■ you are over 25 years old at the beginning of the academic year
■ you have been married before the start of the academic year
■ you have supported yourself during the three years prior to the beginning of the academic year
■ you have no living parents.

If you are an 'independent' student and married, you and your wife, husband or partner will be expected to contribute, depending on your income.

Part-time students

Those studying part-time can apply for non-repayable assistance towards the cost of their tuition fees but this depends on whether you have been in HE before and on your income. Currently, part-time students should apply directly to the university or college to receive this support but there are plans to change this from 2004, when you would apply for the means-tested fee support through your LEA.

There is no upper age limit for applying for help with tuition fees.

In Scotland, the situation is different. Full-time and part-time students who wish to study in a Scottish university or college of HE and fulfil eligibility requirements are exempt from tuition charges.

Living costs

Help with living costs comes from:

- student loans
- other grants, tax credits or bursaries for specific groups
- extra help from your university or college.

Other sources of income for mature students include:

- partner/family contributions
- bank overdrafts
- earnings from work
- charities/sponsorships/scholarships
- benefits for specific groups e.g. single parents
- savings.

Student loans

Most students have to rely on student loans in order to meet their living expenses while in HE. These loans are administered by the Student Loans Company (SLC) and are paid three times a year. Seventy-five per cent of the loan is not means tested and the other 25 per cent is dependent on income. Loans are repayable after completion of studies once you are in employment and earning more than £10,000 per year. There are plans to increase this threshold to £15,000 from April 2005.

To be eligible for a student loan, you must be under 55 years old, and if aged between 50 and 54, you must indicate your intention of returning to work after you graduate.

Full-time students studying outside London in 2003/4 can borrow up to £4,000 per year, while those studying in London are eligible for up to £4,930. The rates for the final year of your course are slightly lower and you can apply for extra if your course is longer than 30 term-time weeks per year.

Part-time students can borrow up to £500 per year at the time of writing this book, but this depends on your income, the income of your partner and if you have dependent children. Part-time initial teacher training students are eligible for the student loan for full-time students.

Among the future changes proposed is an intention to:

■ introduce a means-tested HE grant of up to £1,000 from 2004
■ stop the part-time student loan from 2004, but give access to help for those who are eligible for fee support via Access to Learning funds (see below) and an LEA grant of £250.

Applying for financial support

You can start this process from the January of the year you intend to start your course. If you apply after the deadlines, there may be a delay in receiving your money for the start of term. If you do not apply at all, you may have to pay full fees for a course and will not have access to student loans. Some of the extra support available is dependent on your having applied for student loans.

Full-time students should follow the steps in the Application Process chart on p. 22. Part-time students should get an application pack direct from the DfES for loans and apply to their university for help with fees.

Student Support Direct is a new service that provides assistance to students via the Internet or telephone. Some LEAs, e.g. Birmingham and Durham, are taking part in a pilot of a new simplified application process in 2003.

If you live in Wales, you may be eligible for the Assembly Learning Grant, which includes top-ups for mature students and help with childcare. Contact your LEA or the National Assembly on 02920 825 831 for more information.

The Application Process		
What to do	**How?**	**When?**
STEP ONE Obtain form HE1 (application for Higher Education Support)	From your local education authority (LEA) or by contacting the Department for Education and Skills (DfES)	From January before your course starts
STEP TWO Return the completed HE1 form	To your LEA not more than four months after the start of the academic year (October), and ideally well in advance of it	By mid March
STEP THREE Complete and return HE2 form	The LEA will then send you form HE2, which asks detailed questions about your financial position. Return it to the LEA who will tell you how much you will need to contribute to fees and how much loan you can apply for. They will send any forms for other grants such as the childcare grant	By mid June
STEP FOUR Apply for your student loan	Apply as early as you can after June to the Student Loans Company for your loan. The form to use will be sent to you by the LEA	After June
STEP FIVE Pay any fees and wait for your loan/ grants	Pay fees to your university or college after you have registered at the start of your course. Your loan /grants will be paid into your bank account	September/October
STEP SIX Apply for any extra help you need	Contact your university financial support office for details	After you have started your course

Extra finance for students with dependent children

This system has been completely reviewed in 2003 and previous grants for students – Dependants' Allowance; School Meals Grant; Lone Parents' Grant; Travel, Books and Equipment Grant; the Additional Dependants' Grant; and the discretionary Access Bursary – have been replaced for 2003/4 see Childcare Support chart on p. 23.

The grants are paid with the student loan at the start of each term, but are not repayable. CTC is paid directly into your bank account weekly or monthly.

Part-time students can apply for help through their university or college and the Access and Hardship Funds (Access to Learning Funds from 2004).

For further details, see the DfES booklet *Childcare Grant and Other Financial Help For Student Parents*, available from the DfES website (under forms and guides) or in paper form from your LEA.

Childcare Support		
New support systems from 2003	**Details**	**How to apply and further information**
Child Tax Credit (CTC)	From September 2003, this replaces the Dependants' Grants for children. If you receive the maximum allowance you can also get free school meals, unless you receive Working Tax Credit.	www.inlandrevenue. gov.uk/taxcredits or call the tax credits helpline on 0845 300 3900
The Parents' Learning Allowance (PLA)	Replaces several existing grants for students with dependent children. It combines the old Travel, Books and Equipment Grant, the Additional Dependants' Grant and the discretionary Access Bursary into one grant of up to £1,300 (at 2003/04 rates). The amount you receive depends on your income.	Apply through your LEA
Childcare Grant	You can apply for 85% of actual costs of up to £135 a week for one child and £200 a week for two or more children. For other types of childcare, you can apply for the PLA and for help from Access and Hardship funds (Access to Learning funds from 2004). You cannot receive a Childcare Grant if you, your husband or wife or partner, receive the childcare element of the Working Tax Credit. From 2003, this grant is no longer reduced for the long vacation.	Apply through your LEA before or during your course

'I hadn't applied for the new Child Tax Credits because I thought you had to be working to get it, but then I had a letter from the university telling me students could apply and it means I've an extra £38 a week for me and my son.'

Anthea Rowe, History, Social History and Education student

Working Tax Credits

Mature students who are working more than 30 hours a week, or 16 hours a week (and are responsible for looking after a child or young person or are disabled), may be able to claim Working Tax Credits. Look on the Inland Revenue website for details: www.inlandrevenue.gov.uk/taxcredits.

Adult Dependants' Grant

You can apply through your LEA for up to £2,280 (2003/4) if you are a full-time student with adult dependants.

Disabled Students' Allowances

If you are a disabled part-time or full-time student, you are eligible for financial support to cover the cost of special equipment necessary for you to carry out your studies and/or a non-medical helper, general extra costs and extra travel costs. The DfES guide *Bridging the Gap* has details and is available from their website (under forms and guides), helpline or textphone or in paper form from your LEA. *Bridging the Gap* is also available on audio tape or in Braille.

Extra travel costs

Full-time students who incur travel costs over £270 as part of their course can apply for extra help from the LEA.

Access to Learning Fund

Support is available through the university or college for students who experience severe financial hardship. From 2004/05 there will be a single source of help available from your university or college the Access to Learning Fund. This will replace the Hardship Loan and the Access and Hardship Fund available in 2003/4. These payments are not repayable. In Wales these are known as Financial Contingency Funds (FCF). Full-time students, as well as some part-time students, can apply for help from the fund.

Currently, under hardship funds, you can apply for amounts from £100 to £3,500. Indications are that similar amounts will be available under the new Access to Learning Fund.

Career Development Loans

If you plan to take a vocational (work-related) course but are not eligible for funding through your LEA, you may be able to obtain a Career Development Loan, which is administered through the DfES. You can apply for loans between £300 and £8,000 for courses that last up to two years (or three years if they include work experience). Repayment of the loan begins one month after the end of the course. For further information, contact the CDL Information Line (0800 585 505) or the website: www.lifelonglearning.dfes.gov.uk/cdl.

Benefits

Some students in higher and further education may be entitled to benefits. These benefits are income related and only people in vulnerable groups such as single parents, student couples with dependent children or disabled people will receive them.

This is a complex subject, so consult your local Jobcentre Plus office (which replaced the Benefits Agency, Jobcentres and Social Security Offices in 2002) for advice on the support you will be entitled to. Further information is on the Jobcentre Plus website: www.jobcentreplus.gov.uk or www.dwp.gov.uk.

'Everyone says you can apply for this and that, but you don't know how it will all work out in the end. In the school holidays, because I'm a single parent I can claim income support but it takes months to come through. So I save up during the year to pay the rent for the summer.'
Jacci Qualters, English and Literary Studies
and Media and Cultural Studies

'At the end of my first year, I didn't know what to do about money for the summer holidays. I rang up friends and eventually realised I should apply for income support as I am a single parent. This was a few weeks into the summer and money was running out!'
Anthea Rowe, History, Social History and Education student

Benefit	Details	Where to apply for it
Housing Benefit	help towards your rent	your local council or Jobcentre Plus office
Income Support	for July and August	Jobcentre Plus office
Job Seeker's Allowance	For July and August for some student couples	Jobcentre Plus office

Charities, trusts and foundations

Some educational charities offer help to mature students. They usually target specific groups e.g. people with disabilities. You can find details of charities through:

- directories e.g. *Grants Register* (Macmillan) *Educational Grants Directory* (Directory of Social Change)
- Educational Grants Advisory Service (EGAS) (Tel: 020 7254 6251) www.egas-online.org.uk)
- Funderfinder – a computer database of charities; access is often available through the university or local public library
- useful website www.scholarship-search.org.uk.

Sponsorship

Some employers sponsor students on university courses. You receive a bursary for the academic year, and are paid a normal salary for the time you work for the company in the holidays. Most sponsorship deals are offered to students in sciences, technology, engineering and business. For further information, look at directories, such as *Students Support Sponsorship Funding Directory* (CRAC/Hobsons), available in most careers services and public libraries.

It may also be worth exploring the possibility of obtaining sponsorship with your current employer, if you have one.

Health professional courses

NHS bursaries are available for all full-time or part-time students on courses such as nursing, midwifery, physiotherapy, chiropody, speech and language therapy and radiography. Tuition fees are paid in full by the NHS. The maintenance grant is not means tested for nursing and midwifery diploma students and is currently £5,432 (£6,382 in London). Extra allowances include the older students allowance for those over 26 years, worth £635. Means-tested bursaries are available for degree and other courses. Further details are on the website: www.doh.gov.uk/hcsmain.htm.

The Student Grants Unit of the NHS sends you a form once you have been offered a place on a course.

Dance and Drama Awards

Dance and Drama Awards are available for some students who attend independent drama colleges on courses for professional dancers, actors or stage managers. Awards are means tested and are currently a maximum of £4,100 (£4,600 in London). Further details are in the booklet *Dance and Drama Awards* from DfES and on the website: www.dfes.gov.uk/dancedrama.

Social Work Bursaries

From 2003/4, new non-means-tested bursaries will be available to students (resident in England) on full-time social work first degree and diploma courses. Administered by the General Social Care Council, bursaries are currently £3,000 for students studying outside London and £3,444 for those in London. Look on the website www.socialworkcareers.co.uk.

Other awards and scholarships

Some universities have extra funds they distribute to students already on courses, such as specific scholarships for certain courses and prizes students can compete for. For details, see the university listings in this directory.

A useful website is www.scholarship-search.org.uk, which allows you to search for awards by university.

The Open University provides some help to those of its students who are reliant on benefits, and operates its own hardship fund. See www.open.ac.uk for details.

Financing preparatory courses for HE

See Chapter Five *Getting in – qualifications and preparation* for details of these courses:

A-levels or equivalent

If you do a part-time course at an adult education centre or college of further education you will have to pay the course fee. However, most LEAs have a policy of waiving or reducing these fees if you are in receipt of state benefits or are disabled.

Access courses

Most access courses are free and are organised so that attendance time does not exceed 16 hours in any one week. This means that if you are reliant on benefits, you maintain your eligibility.

Finance Summary	
What to do	**Who to contact**
Get up to date information on student finance from DfES	www.dfes.gov.uk/studentsupport
Contact your LEA as early as you can in the year you start your course. Complete and return forms as requested	The LEA where you live before going to university
Use Student Support Direct – a new service giving assistance to students	Details on DfES website
Contact the local council regarding Council Tax exemptions and Housing Benefit	The local council where you study
Contact the Inland Revenue regarding Tax Credits, if applicable	www.inlandrevenue.gov.uk/taxcredits
Contact the financial support office in your university once you have started regarding any support from Hardship (Access to Learning funds from 2004) or any access to special bursaries in that university. Some Students' Unions have specialist advisers on finance and some will give you advice before you start your course	Your university or college
Contact Jobcentre Plus if you think you will be able to claim any benefits	www.jobcentreplus.gov.uk
Look on websites such as the National Union of Students or support4learning for extra tips	www.nusonline.co.uk. www.support4learning.org.uk

'I found out about the access course by phoning the college. I'm a single parent so I needed to apply to the nearest local college. It was well publicised that there would be no fees for someone like myself and this was important.'

Anne Chammings, Access course student

Foundation courses

Students on foundation courses are entitled to apply for student loans.

'I did the foundation course so I could apply for a student loan a year earlier. In retrospect this was stupid as I now have four years of student loan to repay – I would have been better off staying on benefits and doing the access course. It looked good at the time because it gave me the assurance of a place at university.'

Jacci Qualters, English and Literary Studies and
Media and Cultural Studies student

Long-term residential college courses

You can apply for a DfES bursary to cover tuition fees and living costs. The bursary for living costs is means-tested. Students living in college outside London can apply for up to £3,255 per year (2003/4).

Other courses e.g. short local courses or correspondence courses

You may well have to pay the fees for these courses, although fees may be reduced or waived if you rely on state benefits.

Student finance – the brighter side

Part-time work

Many institutions have 'job-shops', advertising local part-time jobs. Universities often suggest a limit of 12–15 hours a week, as studies have shown that more than this an be detrimental to your coursework.

Student concessions

Concessions are available to students in various ways:

- exemptions from paying Council Tax (subject to certain conditions)
- banks usually offer free overdrafts and banking facilities
- free or reduced-cost dental and optical care
- many shops, cinemas, theatres, leisure centres, etc. make reduced charges to students
- discount on rail fares for full-time students
- insurance and travel companies provide services exclusively for students
- most universities and colleges have a range of shops, canteens and bars on campus that sell goods at lower prices than on the high street.

'One thing I have as a student is more time – at work I was doing 60–70 hours a week and had no time to seek out bargains etc. Now I have and am always on the lookout to make the most of student discounts. I don't believe in paying full price for virtually anything – a bit of forethought saves small amounts, which all add up.'

Steve Noake, Art and Design student

ACCOMMODATION

If you have to move away to attend university you need to do a fair bit of research on what accommodation is available. You will want answers to some of the following questions:

Accommodation tips

- If no university rooms are available, try to make early arrangements if at all possible. You could visit the area during the summer to search for a private room. It may be possible to stay temporarily in a university room in July and August. Contact the university or college housing or accommodation office for information on this point and to obtain a list of suitable vacancies in the private sector.
- Often, mature/professional people contact the university housing officer asking particularly for mature students to share their facilities with. If you like the idea of a quieter environment, this may appeal.
- Rents in private rooms can vary enormously. You can reduce your costs by being flexible. Sharing bathroom and kitchen facilities is cheaper than renting your own self-contained flat. If you have your own transport and are prepared to live further away from the campus, you may find the rents are cheaper.

> **?**
>
> Does the university guarantee a room for all new students?
>
> If so, are specific flats set aside for mature students or will you be happy to share facilities with younger students?
>
> Are there likely to be family flats available?
>
> What is the availability of private rented places?
>
> What is the range of rents?

■ If you do rent in the private sector, you will need to put aside money for a deposit.

'I applied in late September so accommodation was a problem – we were given a list of hotels because the university had nothing for married couples. Eventually, we went through an agency and found a house to live in. The agency's concern is: you're a student – how are you going to pay? We were in a lucky position of making money on the house we sold and we used some of it for a deposit for accommodation. It was the only reason we were accepted by the agency – if it wasn't for that, I don't know how we would have managed.'

Kevin Boreham, Business Management student

To help with your research look at:

■ *The Student Book*, Boehm and Lees-Spalding (Trotman), which indicates universities' policies on accommodation and price ranges
■ the university listings in this directory.

CHILDCARE

If you have school age or pre-school children, affordable safe childcare is essential so you can enjoy and concentrate on your studies. Many universities have childcare facilities for the under fives and some have school holiday provision for those of school age. For details, see the university listings in this directory.

Childcare costs vary across the country, so check with your local Childcare Information Service. Look at the Childcare Link website www.childcarelink.gov.uk or telephone 08000 96 02 96. Example costs include:

- 'out of school clubs' are variable, ranging from £15–50 per child per week
- holiday playschemes vary between £35–90 per week
- childminders usually charge between £2.00 and £4.00 per hour
- university nurseries for under fives. At the University of Birmingham, for students who are eligible for maximum subsidies, rates are nearly £9 per half day, but education nursery grants are available for three and four year olds and there are reductions the more half day sessions are attended. The University of Wolverhampton has a nursery that charges £1.00 per hour to students. Nursery places are in demand and often involve joining a waiting list.

For details on the grants for which you can apply, see the section on Financial Issues.

Childcare arrangements can affect your studies in other ways:

'I can only really choose modules with morning lectures for my degree. Afternoon lectures are from 2–5 and as a single parent with three school age children I have to get back home in the afternoon – a half-hour drive away. School holidays never coincide with your holidays. What do I do with the children for a whole week when I have lectures, then a couple of weeks later I have a whole week off for reading week?'
                                        Jacci Qualters, English and Literary Studies and
                                                    Media and Cultural Studies student

'Having a supportive partner is very important. My husband is self-employed and can work flexible hours, so we took a decision that my studies would have priority for the next few years. I travel 20 miles to university by car, but as my husband works locally, it means one of us is on hand for the children. With six children, studying full time and the travelling, I am busy – there aren't enough hours in the day.'
                                                            Julie Turley, Law student

'As a single parent, I had to choose an access course that was available locally. The hours of the course – over four days – was also important as I had childcare to consider.'

Anne Chammings, Access student

THE NEW YOU – THE EFFECT ON YOU AND YOUR HOME LIFE

Mature students and their families have to make frequent adjustments during the time they are in education. Because some courses assume a significant amount of private study, normal family and social routines can be disrupted. This often creates tensions, which can put pressure on relationships.

'Being a mature student can put a strain on the home life and this is not always foreseen. We had a student who borrowed some expensive textbooks from the library and came home to find her husband had set fire to them!'

University lecturer quoted in 'Moving Forward' p 6. Leicestershire LSC

If you decide to become a mature student, you are making a major commitment. You need to be confident that you will cope with study on top of your current commitments. Also it would make good sense to consider how much support you can expect from your family.

'Being a mature student means I lead two different lives. One minute I am thinking about a complex aspect of jurisprudence, and the next I am sorting the potato alphabet shapes out to spell the children's names. The way I am treated is different too – at home I'm Mum, who sorts out washing and meals, and at university I'm a student like any other.'

Julie Turley, Law student

'Studying was hard – I had a one-year-old daughter when I started, worked part-time in a pub and studied on a full-time degree course. There was a battle between spending the time studying, working and with my family. But the degree has stood me in good stead and I wouldn't be in my present job as an IT lecturer without it.'

Clare Dain, IT and Combined Studies graduate

> **?**
>
> Do you enjoy participating in discussions and arguments?
>
> How do you react to criticism?
>
> How would you feel about working on your own a great deal?
>
> How would you feel about being responsible to yourself, and yourself only, for the amount and quality of the work you do?
>
> Would you find it difficult to organise your own study timetable?
>
> How would you feel about spending a lot of time with people who are in general younger than yourself?
>
> How would you feel about being taught by tutors who may be younger than you?
>
> Would you enjoy spending a lot of time reading?
>
> How did you react to the last major change in your life?

'Balancing work, college and a family has been difficult. But I was determined to do it and I've had support from my husband. I study four days at college, work five evenings in an engineering factory and have a family to consider. Tutors at college have always been helpful and understanding with assignments at busy times.'

Cathy Hinton, Access course student

How will study affect you?

Some students study at home on their own by 'distance learning' or correspondence course, but for most, becoming a student means entering a new social situation and encountering many new people. Most mature students, after a few initial doubts and worries, flourish in their new setting. But you might like to reflect on how quickly you would adapt to your new situation:

CHAPTER FOUR

IS RETURNING TO EDUCATION FOR YOU?

> ## Key Points
>
> ■ Now is the time to consider your reasons for wanting to do it and what you will gain, before you think about how to apply or where to study.
>
> ■ If your sole reason for studying is to enhance your career prospects, look carefully before you choose a course.

This chapter aims to help you reflect on the information you have absorbed so far to assess if returning to education is for you.

The decision to re-enter education is ultimately an act of faith in yourself and your abilities. In order that your faith in yourself is justified, you must be aware of what you are taking on and assess whether going back to education is a realistic option for you.

?

Why do you want to be a student?
What have you got to offer?
What will you gain?
What will happen afterwards?

WHY DO YOU WANT TO BE A STUDENT?

> *'Most research on motivation in continuing education suggests that there are three main, overlapping motives for engaging in learning – vocational, academic and personal interest and development.'*
>
> McNair (1996), quoted in Benn, R., Elliott, J. and Whaley, P. 'Educating Rita and her Sisters', p.24

Mature students re-enter education for a variety of reasons. It is worthwhile giving some thought to identifying your own reasons as this will:

- enable you to assess whether you are likely to maintain the necessary level of interest in your chosen course
- be of immense value when you actually come to the application and interviews for courses.

?

Do you want to follow an interest in a particular subject in depth over such a long period of time?

Do you want to prove to yourself (and possibly others) that you can be successful at this level?

Do you want to obtain qualifications to enter a specific career, or perhaps progress in your existing work?

Do you need a stimulus in your life, perhaps because you have spent years at home looking after a family, or are unemployed?

Are you looking for a new direction because you have reached a crossroads in your life, such as divorce, bereavement or moving house?

Do you have other reasons?

'I didn't feel ready for university at the age of 19, although I had a place to go to in Jamaica. Then I came to England, had my son and decided to have a go. I certainly don't regret it as I see it as a way of building a future for myself and my son.'

Anthea Rowe, History, Social History and Education student

'I decided to retrain to better myself and to gain a qualification and do something more worthwhile than what I am doing now. After nine years in an engineering factory in quality control, I feel as though I've got as far as I can go. The time was right to make the change. With nursing, there's scope and hopefully I can move up the ladder as time goes on.'

Cathy Hinton, Access course student

WHAT HAVE YOU GOT TO OFFER?

More than you might think at first!

Mature applicants tend to undervalue the skills and disciplines learnt in their daily lives at home and in the workplace, and underestimate the relevance of their accumulated life experiences. A useful exercise could be to examine and list your own strengths. Here are some starter questions: Universities benefit from having mature students in their classes:

> *'Mature students always sign up for tutorials that are offered. They are anxious, very often without need, and need a lot of reassurance. Most lecturers find mature students engage with the subject, do the reading and contribute immensely in class. The other real boon is that the top grades every year go to mature students. Proportionally, the number of mature people getting firsts is higher than for younger students – a reflection of their commitment and the energy they put into their studies.'*
>
> *Dr Jill Terry, English Lecturer*

> **?**
>
> Am I organised in my work?
> Have I developed self-discipline at home and/or work?
> What writing skills do I have?
> Do I enjoy discussing issues with other people?
> What are my interests? Why am I interested in them?
> Do I work well as part of a team?
> Have I learnt to work independently?
> Do I have the ability to adapt and change as
> circumstances demand?
> What have I learned from running a home or bringing
> up children?

WHAT WILL YOU GAIN?

> *'What have I gained? How long have you got! Confidence is the first thing. I wondered if I could and now I realise I can. I always was*

methodical but in recent years in a very small environment, and inserting those skills in a wider context was very good for my confidence. From my role as Mature Students Officer in the Students' Union, I've gained a great deal. Working within that education framework has developed my negotiation skills meeting mature students in other institutions on national conferences.'

Pat Tromans, English and History student

'I think principally one of the main things I have gained so far is the concept of arguing a position – taking a balanced viewpoint, backing it up, supporting it with evidence. I feel I'm less opinionated and more willing to see several points of view. I see my current education more than just banking up greater knowledge. I feel this is more rounded and the skills feed into all areas of life.'

Steve Noake, Art and Design student

WHAT WILL HAPPEN AFTERWARDS?

Job prospects

Some mature students decide to study to enhance their chances of gaining satisfying, better paid employment after they graduate. Some succeed in realising these aspirations. Others continue to work in similar areas of work as before, especially when they first graduate, but hope to progress in time. Others do the degree for personal satisfaction and any scope for career enhancement afterwards is a bonus.

Although it is difficult to generalise, the chance of getting into some sectors of employment is greater than others for a mature graduate. Some sectors, such as nursing, social work and other public sector jobs, welcome mature entrants. Other areas are more difficult to enter, or demand unrealistic long hours or mobility across the country. For example, in advertising, and media related occupations, it is more difficult to gain entry over the age of 30. Some areas of work usually require further study after a first degree, e.g. journalism, so find out if your chosen career needs further training and how long this will take.

This situation will hopefully ease when the new age discrimination laws come into effect in 2006.The details are as yet uncertain, but the new legislation will mean employers will not be able to discriminate against you because of your age when you are applying for jobs. There are several websites covering the latest developments:

- The Employers Forum on Age: www.efa.org.uk.
- Agepositive – a government information website: www.agepositive.gov.uk.

'I had a career idea in mind when I came to university: I wanted to go into child counselling or child psychology of some kind. But my ideas and my expectations changed over time. I learnt a lot about myself at university: what I'm good at and what I can do. I walked out with a first class honours degree and assumed people would just give me a job! After graduating, I was unemployed for six months and then I was temping for six months. Then I worked as a research assistant in the Psychology department at University College Worcester. I did data entry and ran experiments. As it was a part-time post, I also took on other roles in administration and as a demonstrator, demonstrating lab sessions with undergraduates. It was very varied, but I saw it as a stepping stone as I planned to do my PhD and to teach. Through doing the demonstrator role, although I enjoyed student contact, I didn't feel I could stand up in front of groups to teach. I then re-evaluated what I wanted to do and realised I wanted to stay in a higher education environment and so I applied for my current job – Information Manager in Student Information and Guidance Services. I've realised I'm suited to this type of job and am really enjoying it at the minute.'

Alison Windsor, 1998 psychology graduate

'I worked as a personal assistant, left to have my first child and went to do an A-level in English as a way of meeting people. My teacher inspired me so much, I looked at her and thought, I want your job. I went on to do an access course, a degree in English, then a PGCE in secondary teaching. After my PGCE, I got part-time work in the FE college. At the same time, I did a part-time MA in English at Warwick and I got part-time teaching at University College Worcester. When I started on my part-time PhD, I gradually did more teaching and then got a full-time lecturer post. It has taken 20 years.'

Dr Jill Terry, English Lecturer

'Doing the degree has made a great change to my life. Before, I was a nursing auxiliary and now I'm working as an IT lecturer at a local FE college. When I first graduated, it took me two months to get my first job as a temporary computer technician with the County Council. From there I moved to work as a network engineer with the Ministry of Defence and then as an IT trainer with a housing association. One thing I've realised is that studying never really stops, as I am now doing a part-time teacher's certificate, which will lead into a PGCE next year.'

Claire Dain, 1998 IT and Combined Studies graduate

'Doing a degree built my confidence a lot and got me my job in the long run. Now I'm doing a job that I would not have been qualified to do before. It wasn't why I studied in the first place and at the age of 50 I thought my career was finished, but now I'm doing a job that's far better than anything I did before.'

Patti Rookes, OU graduate and now Wyre Forest
Lifelong Learning Networks Support Officer

Improving your chances

If you have specific career goals in mind:

- check these out with a careers or guidance service. Check that the advice is impartial, confidential and independent
- if the career you have in mind has a professional body e.g. chiropody, check that the course you fancy is accredited/approved by them
- ask for details of what happened to graduates from the course you are considering
- think about any restrictions you may have, e.g. location, and do your research with this in mind.

Useful information on graduate career related issues:

www.prospects.ac.uk
www.doctorjob.com
Occupations (Connexions)
Penguin Careers Guide (Penguin)

'Workwise, doing a degree increases your prospects of getting a better salary and more opportunities generally. I chose this course because the subjects offered interested me and because most of my experience is in office/secretarial work – I wanted to do something related to my previous background. I'm now thinking of something more financial and believe that studying again has helped me to identify my strengths and weaknesses, as well as more specific interests. I have picked up a few things in the Careers Centre to start learning about the different careers that are available. I think it is down to the individual to make the most of their talents. I know that I am a bit older but I do have work experiences that will be an extra advantage. I have spoken to people at business skills seminars about this and employers have been positive.'
Robyn Budge, Commerce student

What can you do to improve your chances of getting into a career you want?

- do some careers research well in advance – this may help you to choose appropriate modules or work placements during your course
- emphasise your experience, showing the advantages of age and maturity
- take a realistic view of the sectors that are more age friendly, such as the public sector
- take advantage of help available to students through your university careers service e.g. help with interview techniques and career decisions.

Although career considerations may be important, it is equally desirable to apply for a course that you enjoy. A degree is no longer an automatic passport to success in a particular career. Graduates today expect to have a wider range of experiences than in the past.

'Mature students often seem to choose their higher education studies with a career in mind. Pre-entry guidance on this issue is so important, or students could start courses and be disappointed with the outcome.'
Julia Dinsdale, Community Liaison Officer

Still feeling positive? Now look at Chapter Five *Getting in – qualifications and preparation* and Chapter Six *Getting in – choosing a course and applying for a place*. If you feel you need further advice at this stage, see the *Introduction* for details on where to get it.

CHAPTER FIVE

GETTING IN – QUALIFICATIONS AND PREPARATION

Key Points

■ If you already have enough qualifications to apply for a degree or course, you may still want to brush up on your study skills.

■ Qualifications are often changing – so always double check that the information you have is up to date.

■ This chapter covers qualifications in England, Wales and Northern Ireland. Qualifications in Scotland have just been reviewed and are different. See www.scqf.org.uk for Scottish information.

This chapter looks at the qualifications needed for entry to HE courses and how you can prepare before you start.

NATIONAL QUALIFICATIONS FRAMEWORK

There is now a National Qualifications Framework for England, Wales and Northern Ireland, which will give you an idea of where any qualifications you hold fit into the system. It may also help you decide on what level of qualification to study as preparation for entry to a HE course. For details see the websites:

■ www.qca.org.uk Qualifications and Curriculum Authority.
■ www.ucas.com UCAS
■ www.edexcel.org.uk Edexcel

In Scotland, a new qualifications framework is being developed for implementation in 2004/5. See the Scottish Credit and Qualifications Framework website for details (www.scqf.org.uk).

National Qualifications Framework (NQF) May 2003

NQF level	Academic awards	General vocational awards	Key and basic skills	Employment-led awards, certificates, diploma	Specialist vocational qualifications	Work-related national vocational qualifications
Entry	Entry level certificate	Entry level certificates in Skills for Working Life and Life Skills	Adult basic skills entry level			
1	GCSE grades D-G	Foundation GNVQ GCSE in Vocational subjects Grades DD-GG	Key Skill Level 1 Adult Basic Skills Level 1	BTEC Foundation		NVQ Level 1
2	GCSE grades A-C* Intermediate FSMQ	Intermediate GNVQ GCSE in Vocational subjects grades A*A*-CC	Key Skill Level 2 Adult Basic Skills Level 2	BTEC Intermediate	BTEC First Diploma	NVQ Level 2
3	A/AS GCE Advanced extension awards (AEA) Advanced FSMQ	Vocational A/AS levels (AVCE/ASVCE/AVCE Double award)	Key Skill Level 3	BTEC Advanced	BTEC Nationals Diploma in Foundation Studies (Art and Design)	NVQ Level 3
4	First Degree Foundation degree		Key Skill Level 4	BTEC Professional	BTEC Higher National Diploma (HND) BTEC Higher National Certificate (HNC)	NVQ Level 4
5	Higher level qualifications Postgraduate degrees		Key Skill Level 5	BTEC Advanced Professional		NVQ Level 5

ARE YOU ALREADY QUALIFIED FOR HE?

Unless the courses you are interested in have 'open access', such as Open University degrees, and do not ask for any qualifications prior to entry, admission to all other HE courses usually requires some qualifications or work experience.

Standard entry

If you passed your exams some time ago, this requirement may not be applied as rigorously; instead your experience and motivation will determine whether or not you are accepted, at least in part. It is still worth understanding how the system works.

For standard entry applicants (those who enter HE directly from school aged 18–20), universities and colleges require Level 3 qualifications before applicants are considered for a place on a degree course or Higher National Diploma (HND). In addition, they require supporting GCSE or equivalent qualifications.

For each course, universities and colleges have:

- general entry requirements e.g. two or three A-levels, a mixture of A-levels and AS levels, a BTEC National Diploma, the International Baccalaureate Diploma, or Access to Higher Education qualification. Some universities also ask for GCSE Grade C or equivalent in maths and English. This may be expressed as a number of units e.g. 18 units, where one full A-level equals 6 units
- course specific entry requirements, where particular subjects have been studied.

Grades and tariff points

Standard entry applicants are required to gain specific grades in their exams. Places are offered on the basis of A-level grades and/or UCAS tariff points. A-level grades are converted into points e.g. grade A = 120 points, grade B =100 points and so on. BTEC qualifications have recently been added to this tariff, and will apply to those who want to enter university courses in 2004. Details are on the UCAS website (www.ucas.com) under curriculum and qualifications.

For mature applicants, universities and colleges have different entry systems and admissions requirements. Many require some evidence that you have studied at Level 3 in the past. For details, see the university listings in this directory. Mature applicants to universities and colleges of HE usually fall into one of four groups and have:

■ academic qualifications – A-levels or equivalent, often taken several years ago
■ professional qualifications
■ directly relevant work experience but no formal qualifications
■ no qualifications or directly relevant work experience.

Academic qualifications

Existing A-levels or equivalent

You have to apply for all full-time courses in HE through a centralised administrative system: the Universities and Colleges Admissions Service (UCAS), and not to individual universities or colleges. You can still contact individual institutions (admissions departments) to check if your existing qualifications are acceptable for certain courses.

> *'I found the admissions office at the university very helpful when I rang to enquire about degree courses. This encouraged me to apply, as they seemed to welcome mature applicants.'*
> Kevin Boreham, Business Management student

A significant minority of mature students is returning to HE after having made a 'false start' at some earlier time. If you are in this situation, you may find your previous learning will be acknowledged when you are considered for a place, and it is unlikely that you will be discriminated against because of your earlier withdrawal.

Remember, qualifying for entry does not necessarily guarantee you a place. Some courses are very competitive, e.g. physiotherapy, law, medicine, psychology, and can be very selective. Others require very specific subjects for entry e.g. physical sciences, such as chemistry, physics and maths. Humanities courses, such as philosophy, arts and social sciences, can usually accept a broader range of qualifications for entry.

The entrance requirements for courses can be found in *Degree Course Offers* (Trotman) (see Chapter Nine *Further Information*) or under the departmental entries in the prospectuses and on university websites. If you have any doubts concerning your eligibility contact the admissions tutor of the department concerned or the admissions officer or registrar of the university or college.

> *'I've got ancient A-levels, which were enough for entry. I didn't do any courses specifically geared towards doing the degree. I had done some IT courses as and when I needed them for my work, which have come in useful.'*
>
> Pat Tromans, English and History student

Professional qualifications

Many mature applicants gain entry to HE on the strength of vocational qualifications they have obtained since leaving school.

If you have such a qualification – for instance, City & Guilds or NVQ etc. – it is worth checking if this will qualify for entry to a degree course. Some institutions are willing to accept such qualifications and others are not. You could contact the admissions staff for the course you are interested in, detailing the exact qualifications. Give as much information as you can, including syllabus details and any official documentation if possible.

No formal qualifications but relevant work experience

Many mature students in HE began the entry procedure with no qualifications to their name. If you are in this situation, a number of options are open to you including preparatory courses you can take.

Sometimes universities and colleges are prepared to interview 'unqualified' applicants if they have demonstrated their suitability for the course on the UCAS application form. They may even offer you a place and waive the need for any further qualifications if they believe that you are sufficiently motivated and capable of doing the course.

Until comparatively recently, knowledge and skills developed at work were unrecognised by universities and colleges, mainly because of the difficulties of assessing them. Now many institutions properly acknowledge such knowledge and skills, and consider them as a valid qualification for acceptance. This process is known as the Accreditation of Prior Experiential Learning (APEL) and is where credit is given for your work or voluntary experience. Some institutions offer an APEL module to help you assemble evidence of such learning.

WHAT COURSES OR EXAMS WILL HELP YOU QUALIFY FOR ENTRY?

'I did A-levels when I was younger, but didn't do very well in them as I was distracted at that time in my life. I went to my local college for an access course, timing it so that I could start a degree course when the twins started school. I also did two A-levels (General Studies and Law) at the same time, partly to get back into studying, and to prove to myself that I could do it.'

Julie Turley, Law student

There are various courses that will help you qualify and get back into the swing of studying again.

Access courses

Access courses are now probably the most popular means of entering HE for prospective students who have no qualifications. They offer people who have been out of education the opportunity to acquire study skills and further their knowledge in a particular area of study.

Accredited access courses are accepted by most universities as general entry requirements, but they will not be necessarily accepted by all courses at those institutions, as each course has both a general entry requirement and a course-specific entry requirement (see above under 'Standard entry').

The time commitment for access courses varies from one or two sessions per week (often available in the evening) over two or three years, to full-time courses over one year. The courses can offer a very supportive environment, help you with writing essays, preparing projects and sitting exams, and filling in your application form for HE. Recently, online access courses have been developed.

Access courses are validated by approved agencies (AVA – Authorised Validating Agencies) who are recognised by the Quality Assurance Agency, the same body that oversees the quality of degree courses in universities and colleges.

'I suggest to people, when they ring up, to contact the universities they are interested in, find out what qualifications they require and if it matches the qualifications we are offering. If they already have enough qualifications to apply for the degree course they want, I suggest they look at all the alternatives before deciding to come on this course – A-level or HND or HNC modules, for example. They often come because access is offering them a whole qualification that will get them into nursing etc. and helps their self-esteem. They like the idea of being with a group of people.'

Jane Tope, Access to Caring Professions tutor

'I looked at going back to do a GNVQ – but access appealed more because I would be with people who would have the same life experiences as me, be more on the same wave length as me. The hours fitted within school times too. At the time, I wanted to go on and study midwifery, but later decided to apply for a psychology degree.' Rebecca Orr, Access course student

Some access courses may be held in colleges that have a relationship with a neighbouring university or college; passing the course may mean a guarantee of an interview, or even a place, at that institution in some cases. These arrangements are relatively rare, and most access courses act as a general 'currency', making you eligible for a variety of HE courses but not guaranteeing a place on any one of them.

Access courses are usually held in local colleges of FE. To find out about the courses that are being run in your area, contact your local college. The UCAS website has further details on courses – www.ucas.com/access. In Scotland, the Scottish Wider Access Programme has details. See www.swap2highereducation.com.

Long-term residential college courses

There are seven colleges that offer residential one or two year full-time courses to adults over 20 years of age who have no previous qualifications. Some are access courses, others certificates of HE, DipHE or foundation years. Each college offers slightly different courses, so you will need to contact each for details. They are Coleg Harlech (Wales), Fircroft College (Birmingham), Hillcroft College (Surrey), Newbattle Abbey College (Dalkeith), Northern College (Barnsley), Plater College (Oxford) and Ruskin College (Oxford). Students apply for a bursary to cover fees and living costs.

They offer the chance for a complete break from your present lifestyle and provide the opportunity to give your full attention to studying in a very supportive environment:

'We offer an intensive learning experience. The learning in the classroom is complemented and enhanced by activities outside the classroom. For example our library and learning resources are open 24 hours a day and there is a series of cultural visits. Students have a personal tutor – a student could see their personal tutor every day if they wanted!'
Fiona Larden, Principal, Fircroft College.

Foundation years

Foundation years are designed to help those without the usual entry requirements to obtain study skills and subject knowledge. You are usually guaranteed a place on Year 1 of the degree course at the same university. Foundation courses can also act as a preliminary introductory year to a specific degree course. Passing a foundation course does not normally entitle you to entry to any course other than the one it is designed for.

Sometimes, the first year or foundation year of a course is 'franchised' out to another institution, such as a college of FE. This may mean that you can do part of your degree at a local institution and only have to attend university in the latter part of the course. Some foundation courses are run alongside access courses where you would study similar topics and modules.

Foundation years are not the same as foundation degrees and should not be confused with art and design foundation studies courses.

Art and design foundation studies courses

One- year art foundation courses, run in FE or specialist art colleges, have been a traditional way of developing skills in the different art and design disciplines before deciding which area, e.g. graphics, 3D, fashion and textiles or fine art, to study at degree level. These courses are technically FE courses and you apply for degrees during this course. A list of these courses is on the UCAS website (www.ucas.com) – use the 'site index' to find a list of courses quickly.

Essay method / entrance exams

In some institutions you may be required to sit an entrance exam of some kind or submit an essay to show your potential for university-level study. These entry methods vary, depending on the course and the institution.

If you gain entry this way, and if you have enough time before the course starts, some kind of preparatory reading or course about study skills will help you settle more quickly into studying. Some students who enter this way can find the first few weeks of study a struggle:

> *They asked me to do a 1,500 word essay on one of three questions and gave me a fortnight to do it. Then I completed a UCAS form. The study I had done previously with the Open University through work helped with this and I did a lot of report writing as part of my job as a technical manager for a furniture company. Once I got over the first few weeks, I found study came quite easily.'*
>
> Kevin Boreham, Business Management student

To prepare for an exam you could:

- attend a short preparatory course, if available
- consult one of the practical books currently available e.g. *Exams Without Anxiety* by David Acres, and *The Good Study Guide* published by Open University Press (see Chapter Nine *Further Information*)

■ obtain copies of the entrance exam papers from previous years by contacting the institution concerned. This will give you a good idea of the type of test questions you will be asked.

Open University (OU) courses

OU courses are frequently used by mature applicants as a qualification for entry to other degree courses. 'Openings' courses can be studied in different subjects and give an insight into HE-level study. The advantage of doing such a course is that the OU is totally geared to the needs of older students who can participate without any significant disruption to their normal lives. All studying can be done by 'distance learning' correspondence, internet, television and radio (although there is some opportunity to meet other students and your tutor later on). See www.open.ac.uk for details.

Taking GCE A-levels (or equivalent)

A-levels are well recognised qualifications that, traditionally, have provided access to HE courses. You can study for A-levels (or other equivalent exams) full-time, part-time, during the day or in the evening:

■ at your local college of FE
■ at your local sixth-form college
■ through correspondence courses, such as those run by the National Extension College
■ some schools now encourage adults to take A-level courses alongside 16 to 18-year-olds.

The A-level system changed in 2000, with the introduction of AS (Advanced Subsidiary) level and A2 (full A-level) courses. Each full A-level consists of six separate units. The first three of these units lead to an AS qualification. Usually the AS level is taken at the end of one year and the full A-level at the end of the second year, although some shorter courses are available. There is a mix of exams and coursework.

Equivalents

There are several courses considered to be equivalent to A-level. Not all university courses will accept A-level equivalent qualifications, so if you have a particular course or university in mind, consult them first before embarking on an 'equivalent' course. They include:

BTEC National courses

Diplomas, certificates and awards are also taught at FE colleges, sixth form colleges and schools and are Level 3 qualifications. They are work-related qualifications in subjects such as business, IT or engineering. New BTEC qualifications started in 2002. The new National Diploma is an 18 unit award and is equivalent to three A-levels and the Certificate to two A-levels (12 units). The BTEC National Award is a six unit award equivalent to one A-level. BTEC National Diplomas awarded before 2002 were 16 (not 18) unit awards, so have a slightly lower equivalence. Further information is on the Edexcel website (www.edexcel.org.uk).

Advanced Vocational Certificate of Education (AVCE)

Previously known as Advanced GNVQs (General National Vocational Qualifications), AVCEs are also referred to as vocational A-levels. They have the same value as conventional A-levels but have a work-related bias e.g. art and design, manufacturing, business, science, information and communication technology, and health and social care. There is more assessed coursework and fewer exams than conventional A-levels, which may appeal to older students.

Scottish National Qualifications

These are new qualifications replacing SCE Highers. Details are on the website – www.sqa.org.uk.

A list of qualifications equivalent to A-level can be found in more detail on the UCAS website – www.ucas.com.

OTHER WAYS TO PREPARE FOR STUDY

Even if you do have the necessary qualifications to enter HE, and decide not to do another A-level or an Access course, you may well feel the need to flex your intellectual 'muscles' before you start. Some mature students lack confidence and worry they will struggle with the level of work. In reality, mature students tend to do very well on degree courses.

Self-preparation

'My degree course starts in 2004 so I will have a gap of a year. In that year before the degree starts I plan on going back to college and doing some more of the Access course – I feel I need to keep my hand in, academically, and I don't want the confidence I've gained in the last year to go stale. At my age I need continual encouragment.'

Anne Chammings, Access course student

You may not have the time to prepare yourself for HE by doing another course. But you could:

■ contact the institution you are hoping to enter and ask for a reading list for prospective students
■ try to join the library of your local college or university on an independent basis.

You may prefer to do this kind of preparation once you have secured a place, but reading some relevant books can be a sound investment if you are called to interview. It is quite common for interviewers to ask about a book you have recently read, so reading something well known or recently published, or that has received some acclaim, is an excellent idea for all prospective students.

Study skills courses

Short study skills courses may be available locally as part of an adult education programme from local education authorities or university lifelong learning departments. Contact your local adult education centre, college or library who should have details of courses available. You could also try the National Extension College for distance learning courses (www.nec.ac.uk). These courses offer preparation for HE through practice in essay writing, note-taking and seminar participation.

See Chapter Two – *What to expect* – for more details on study skills.

GCSEs and other assessed courses

Some students may have to register for GCSE courses in English language and mathematics, if they do not already have them, to be eligible for entry to some courses. They (or equivalents) are essential for those who want to eventually become teachers. Others just want to extend their knowledge of a subject because it is related to what they will study in the future.

Alternatives to GCSEs are BTECs and GNVQ intermediate or foundation courses, which are available in a range of subjects.

Contact your local FE college for details or the Learndirect website (www.learndirect.co.uk).

Computer courses

You will be expected to word-process your assignments, and the Internet will be an invaluable tool in your research. There are many inexpensive or free courses available in several locations, from local colleges to community centres. If you have some computing experience already, a course in touch-typing, some of which can be obtained on CD-ROM, will be a great time saver. The Learndirect website (www.learndirect.co.uk) can advise on courses in your area.

See Chapter Two – *What to expect* – for more details of why IT skills are important preparation for HE.

Associate student schemes / test modules

Increasingly, colleges and universities are opening up a variety of their courses to the general public. You can attend classes alongside regular students; in some cases your work is assessed, in others it is not. You do normally have to pay to participate on one of these schemes, but it is an ideal way to get a realistic feel for what student life is like. You can do such a course as a 'one off', and you may find that you can use any credit you gain towards a qualification if you decide to go on studying at that institution.

Community programmes

Short courses to encourage adults to return to learning are available in most parts of the country. They could be run in FE colleges or in local community centres.

A FINAL THOUGHT

Even if you do have the necessary qualifications at the grades required, there is no guarantee that you will be offered a place. This simply reflects the fact that places on some courses in HE are in short supply and does not necessarily imply that your qualifications are inadequate.

If you do get turned down, you can try to find out why by contacting the admissions staff (or the mature students' adviser if there is one). You may then be able to remedy the situation and apply again the following year.

If you need further help with deciding which courses are appropriate to help you qualify for a HE course, see the *Introduction* for details on where to get further advice.

CHAPTER SIX

GETTING IN – CHOOSING A COURSE AND APPLYING FOR A PLACE

Key Points

- Get advice from several sources to help you make the right decision.
- Visit the university or college and gather all the information you can before choosing where to apply.
- Apply early, if at all possible, to increase your chances of getting a place on the course you want.
- Apply though UCAS for full-time courses and directly to the university for part-time or distance learning courses.

This chapter covers the practicalities of choosing a course, deciding on which university or college to go to, and how to apply though UCAS.

Throughout this book, there are references to agencies, books and websites that can give you more detail on where to get further advice. It is especially important to check the information you have is up to date and accurate.

If you want to talk over the options, try to ensure the guidance you get is impartial. If that is not possible, get several points of view before making a decision that could so drastically affect your life. See the *Introduction* for more details on where to get further advice.

CHOOSING A COURSE

'Do a lot of research before you choose your course unless you are really certain which course you want to go on. There are a lot of courses out

*there and you have got to be happy in what you are doing because it
needs a lot of commitment.'*

Penny, English and Literary Studies student

A glance at UCAS course information shows a bewildering array of choices
in HE. There are currently 55,000 courses on offer at 330 institutions. If
you decide to study full-time and apply through UCAS you are allowed up
to six choices on the application form – how do you make a selection?

To assist you in making the right choice, consider these four questions:

> **?**
>
> Where to study?
> How to study?
> What to study?
> What are your personal needs?

WHERE?

*'I was living in Crawley and I wanted to study a particular course. After
going through the UCAS book I discovered only about 12 places did this
particular course. Some were discounted because of size and some
because of cost of living. I needed to move anyway as I had been made
redundant and could no longer pay the mortgage. Living in Worcester
was cheaper than Crawley and the university was very helpful when I
rang up to enquire.'*

Kevin Boreham, Business Management student

*'I decided I was going to go to university the year before, so I got
prospectuses from all the local universities and made my choices early.
Living in Staffordshire meant I had a wide range of universities to
choose from within reasonable commuting distance. I found applying
though UCAS quite easy and straightforward, even though I'm
Canadian and had to learn about the education system here.'*

Robyn Budge, Commerce student

If you decide you want to attend a course, as opposed to doing distance
learning, research carefully all the available options. Many older applicants

have constraints on where they can apply. Some applicants with children, for example, cannot travel far and consequently there may be only one or two institutions that are realistic options for them. Consider these issues:

> **?**
>
> Are you confined to your locality?
> Can you travel daily?
> How far is acceptable?
> Could you live away from home during the week?
> Could you live away from home during the term?
> Could you move to a new locality altogether?

The accessibility of universities and colleges is, in practice, often dependent on travel facilities; a decent train service can make somewhere 40 miles away a possibility, but if you have to rely on an infrequent bus service, a comparatively short distance may be a nightmare. You can study some courses for a year or two at a local FE college and finish them at the university further away.

Some universities have more than one campus. Most students are based at one of the sites, but some travel, especially for central services or libraries, may be needed. For details see the university listings in this directory.

HOW AND WHAT TO STUDY

See Chapter One – *What's on offer* – for details of types of courses available at universities and colleges of HE. The main questions to ask are:

Vocational or non-vocational course?

Do you want the course to qualify you for a particular job, e.g. nursing, or a subject you have an academic interest in with less vocational direction e.g. English?

> *'The whole aim of doing this course was to get a job in what I wanted to do – midwifery – and I just hadn't got round to it before. I didn't want to do a degree and not know what I wanted to do with it. I applied to*

the local university for practical reasons – I have just moved back to this area from Bristol 18 months ago and I want to stay and work in this area after the course.'

Polly Stephen, Access student

Combined or single subject degrees?

You may prefer doing a degree in more than one subject, especially if you are uncertain about what you are good at or are unclear about your interests.

Work experience / sandwich courses?

Some institutions provide work experience as part of the degree programme. This can form a large part of the course – a year in the case of most sandwich courses. There may also be a number of compulsory courses that are work related in some way, or there might be opportunities to acquire work experience or short vocational courses. Do you want to get off the treadmill of work for a short period or could this be useful to your future career?

Methods of assessment?

If you are not good at exams you could look for courses available that are assessed in other ways, at least for part of the course.

'I was limited in my choice of university by my husband's work; moving house was not an option. Fortunately the local university had a modular course that was perfect for me. I could build up good marks from coursework alone and reduce the pressure during exams (which I hate almost as much as spiders and housework). This is the first tactic – if you hate exams, look for coursework based courses; if you hate coursework look for exam dominated courses. You know your own preferences so don't be pressured into applying for a course you know won't suit you.'

S. Anderton (1998), How I got my First Class Degree, P. Tolmie, p. 68

Part-time, full-time or more flexible course?

You may find that during your course your circumstances change. If you think changes will occur, look for courses and universities that have a more flexible approach to changing how you study part-way through the course. For details of flexible learning opportunities, see the university listings in this directory.

PERSONAL NEEDS

See Chapter Eight *When you get there* for details on mature student support. Mature students' officers are employed by some universities to give support to their students. The greater the number of mature students at a university, the greater the chance of more extensive mature student support. For details, see the university listings in this directory.

Special needs support

Students with disabilities of all kinds currently study successfully at all levels of education. There is a variety of support available for those who need it, including: specially adapted accommodation, personal assistance, computer-aided technology, note-takers, BSL (British Sign Language) translators, hearing loops, etc. The needs of people with mental health difficulties of all kinds are now being recognised and addressed by educational institutions.

> *'I got hardly any qualifications at school. I'm one of those cases where I was dyslexic but no one recognised it back in the '60s. Even now aged 42 I still feel vulnerable and feel it is something that is frowned upon. I have had such support since I have been doing this access course, as it's now considered to be as commonplace as if I'm right- or left-handed. I didn't tell them when I applied to do the Access course because I wasn't comfortable with it but I needed to tell them at the interview for my midwifery degree because I had to do an essay.'*
>
> Anne Chammings, Access student

Changes in the law have led to more enlightened policies and support for disabled students. It is now the responsibility of institutions to make reasonable adjustments to prevent any disadvantage for disabled students. Many colleges and universities now employ disability coordinators who help to provide appropriate support to those who require it.

Despite this, some institutions are still developing their services and may still have much to learn. If you are disabled, you are advised to contact all the institutions that appeal to you, indicating the nature of your disability and any special arrangements you may need regarding your studies, daily living and accommodation. It will be easier for you and for everybody else if arrangements are in place before you start your course, particularly as you will have plenty to cope with when you arrive in any case!

Skill – the National Bureau for Students with Disabilities – is an organisation that provides information and advice to disabled students as well as applicants to further and higher education. (www.skill.org.uk.)

The Disabled Students' Guide to University (Trotman) lists information by university with contact details for disability officers.

Sexuality

Most universities and colleges have LGB (Lesbian, Gay and Bisexual) societies. They are usually run through the students' union and provide both social opportunities and advice about the local area.

Race and religion

Universities are multicultural organisations, with students and staff from a range of backgrounds. Usually there is a wide range of societies you can join through the students' union. The university chaplains organise religious facilities. Many universities also employ an ethnic minority officer or equal opportunities officer to consult if there are problems.

'I am really enjoying university. Birmingham is a big university and one of the main things I like is that it is such an opportunity to meet people from different religions, cultures, ages - all from different parts of the world.'
Julie Turley, Law student

Recent research suggests that for some students the presence of other ethnic minority students is a factor when choosing a university. Students involved in the research comment:

'I did read about the African Caribbean societies and the Asian societies and all the different things they do... It means you know you're not going to be the only black person there.'

> *'I wanted to go somewhere where there were other Asian students…*
> *Most of the universities I have chosen have Islamic Societies…'*
> **Ethnic Choosing: Minority Ethnic Students, Social Class**
> **and Higher Education Choice** (Ball, Reay and David 2002)

If this is an important issue for you, contact the university or college for further information.

ARRANGE A VISIT

The place where you study is of key importance and will largely determine the quality of the experience you will enjoy there. When choosing you may need to consider:

- study support services
- the availability of childcare facilities
- the proportion of mature students
- the availability and cost of accommodation
- the atmosphere of the institution
- the friendliness of staff and students and the physical setting
- the amount of mature student support.

Apart from the factual information about childcare and accommodation (see Chapter Three *Issues to consider*), some aspects cannot really be judged from prospectuses, and it is advisable to visit the institution and talk to other students to get a better feeling for the general ambience of the place. Most institutions offer open days that enable you to look around. UCAS gives details of such events.

Look out for events open to the general public – concerts, exhibitions, fairs and public lectures. Universities often arrange events the public can attend, or have museums or art galleries you can visit.

> *'Students should look at the number of mature students in a university.*
> *It doesn't mean you are going to get on with them, but is often a*
> *reflection of how flexible the university is regarding hours. This is*
> *assuming there is a choice – in some parts of the country there is only*
> *one institution possible. If you are thinking of moving away, think about*
> *the accommodation there is for mature students – you may find living in*

a hall with a lot of 18 year olds very difficult. Talk to the students at open days.'

Rose Watson, Pre-entry advice and guidance worker

'If you are going to visit a university, go with a list of questions as it is easy to get distracted when you get there. Finding out who to talk to about different issues (admissions, finance, course details etc.) is sometimes difficult, so be patient and try to find the right person to ask.'

Julia Dinsdale, Community Liaison Officer

APPLYING FOR A PLACE

For **full-time** degree courses or sandwich courses or HNDs at universities and colleges of HE, you have to apply through a central administrative system – UCAS (Universities and Colleges Admissions Service). For nursing diplomas, apply through a different admissions system – details are on the UCAS website (www.ucas.com).

For **part-time** or distance learning courses, you apply directly to the university or college.

'I applied directly to the college and got an interview. I started in January, so I don't remember completing a UCAS form, I just brought my A-level certificates. It was very informal.'

Pat Tromans, part-time English and History student

'The UCAS form wasn't too bad. The personal statement was the worst thing because you have to get a lot of information on it and give it a positive tone – it was difficult trying to sell yourself appropriately. Anything I'm not sure about I ask the Access tutor to help with.'

Polly Stephen, Access student

THE UCAS APPLICATION PROCEDURE

UCAS publishes a very useful booklet: *The Mature Student's Guide to Higher Education*. If you are currently on an FE course, a copy will be available to you through the college. See Chapter Nine *Further information* for UCAS's address or contact them through their website (www.ucas.com).

Applications can be submitted from September onwards in the year before you intend to begin your studies. **Send off your application as early as possible** – UCAS operates on a 'first come, first served' basis. If your application is late (after mid-January) don't be put off – you still stand a chance, but not necessarily on the course of your choice. Procedures for applying for art and design courses are different, so consult the UCAS website for details.

UCAS APPLICATION SYSTEM

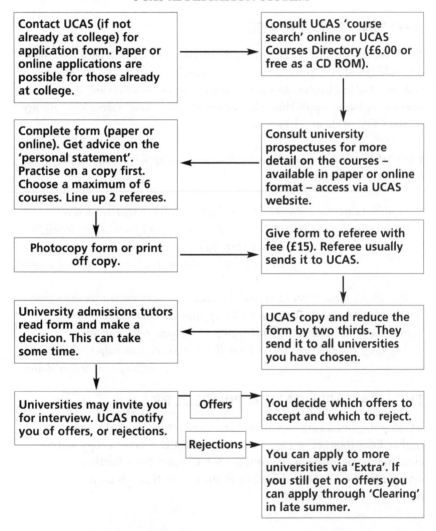

Contact UCAS (if not already at college) for application form. Paper or online applications are possible for those already at college. → Consult UCAS 'course search' online or UCAS Courses Directory (£6.00 or free as a CD ROM).

Complete form (paper or online). Get advice on the 'personal statement'. Practise on a copy first. Choose a maximum of 6 courses. Line up 2 referees. ← Consult university prospectuses for more detail on the courses – available in paper or online format – access via UCAS website.

Photocopy form or print off copy. → Give form to referee with fee (£15). Referee usually sends it to UCAS.

University admissions tutors read form and make a decision. This can take some time. ← UCAS copy and reduce the form by two thirds. They send it to all universities you have chosen.

Universities may invite you for interview. UCAS notify you of offers, or rejections.

Offers → You decide which offers to accept and which to reject.

Rejections → You can apply to more universities via 'Extra'. If you still get no offers you can apply through 'Clearing' in late summer.

'When they fill in this UCAS form and they do the personal statement some students feel it is more difficult than doing some of their assignments. We give them one credit for just going through the process – an 'Applying to Higher Education' unit. It encourages them to evaluate their own performance.'

Jane Tope, Access to Caring Professions tutor

'I encourage our mature students to use positive action words to describe their own experiences. This is particularly (but not exclusively) important for vocational courses; words such as 'produced/observed/analysed/discussed' reinforce you as an individual who can critically evaluate your experiences. You then need to match this to your chosen institutions' general course requirements ... Look to make an effective use of key linking sentences such as 'Having taken part in... has enabled me to...'. In doing so you should have a personal statement that is coherent, comprehensive and organised'.

(The Mature Student's Guide to Higher Education 2003)

Personal statement

This is an important section on the form. In about three quarters of a page you have to sell yourself, explain your background and your reasons for wanting to enter HE. Include any information that might make you stand out from other applicants, and that could act as a 'trigger' for questions if you are called for interview. There is no magic formula for completing this section, but the following suggestions may be helpful:

- use all the space
- try to be original. The most common opening sentence is, 'I've always wanted to study...' so try to be different
- take up about half of the space with course related issues – reasons why you want to do the course
- comments about your work experience, interests and skills are important, but try and make them relevant to the course you are applying for. You can see what skills you need to do well on a course from the 'entry profiles' for each course on the UCAS website. Use these profiles to help you decide what to include on the personal statement. Describe the skills you have gained from your life

experiences. For instance, one woman wrote about the skills learnt from her being a single mother, including effective time management

- avoid repeating material elsewhere on the form
- consider dividing the section into headings: reasons for choosing the course, paid or unpaid work, interests etc
- explain why you finished with education before and why you now wish to return. This is especially useful if you have previously studied in HE and withdrew for some reason
- be specific about your interests. This gives the reader a better idea of you as a person, and provides some material to discuss during an interview. So, rather than state that you 'enjoy reading', say what type of books interest you – for instance, women's writing or science fiction
- UCAS suggests mentioning future plans, but if you do not have a particular goal in this area, don't worry. You can say either that you don't have any special ambitions at this stage, or leave it out altogether.

WHAT HAPPENS NEXT?

If you use the paper form to apply, once received, UCAS copy it (reduced by two thirds) and send it to all the universities on your list. Every year UCAS receives forms that are not completed correctly, slowing down the process. In 2003 they received 15,000 forms with the wrong date of birth!

UCAS do not decide if you will get a place. The university admissions tutors in the universities decide if you will receive:

- an offer of a place without interview
- an interview
- a rejection.

This may take some time and you may have to wait several weeks or months before you hear from each university.

INTERVIEWS

Preparing for the interview

Many institutions no longer interview applicants. Others do not interview those applying directly from school but sometimes interview mature candidates. For details, see the university listings in this directory. If you are asked to attend an interview, it will usually be some months after you have sent off your application form, often between November and March. Before the interview you can prepare yourself:

- re-read the photocopy of your UCAS form
- re-read the prospectus – you need to convince the interviewer that you really want to study at that institution
- are you familiar with the subject matter? Especially if you are doing a subject that you have not studied before, make sure that you can define what the subject is and have a reasonable idea of the kinds of topics you would be addressing on the course
- do you know where you are going? Some institutions are spread over several sites, sometimes miles apart. If you are in any doubt about where you should go, or if you need overnight accommodation, phone the institution for information
- clothing – applicants wear a variety of items to interviews, from jeans and sweatshirts to three-piece suits. The best advice is to wear what you feel comfortable in and, if in doubt, err on the conservative side but look as if you have made an effort
- you may find a rehearsal helpful. Practise your responses to typical questions with friends or a tutor
- consider what qualities universities are looking for. Look at the subject profiles on the UCAS website, which usually list the skills they think are important for the course. When asked which factors influence their assessment of interviewees, admissions tutors usually list the following:

Skill	Examples of evidence
Motivation	examples of your interest in and a commitment to the subject
Relevant work, domestic or leisure experience	an appreciation of how it relates to the proposed studies
Ability to communicate	expressing yourself effectively in writing and in speech, the willingness to listen, and a readiness to work in groups
Organisational skills	whether it be the ordering of ideas and tasks or time management
Potential	evidence of recent achievement, for instance on an access or other preparatory course; signs of initiative and imagination

At this stage the interviewer is not looking for detailed knowledge of the subject area or specific academic skills.

The interview

Interviews can take different forms – from a half-hour with an admissions tutor or lecturer from the course to a whole day event where they set different exercises. Most days will include an individual interview, but not all.

> 'Interviews vary a lot. For example, for social work they have different styles of assessing candidates. I have known students to have:
> – an interview and give a presentation
> – an interview and take part in a debate e.g. for and against euthanasia
> – written tasks instead of an interview e.g students summarise a section of an academic text book (sent in advance of the interview) and an unseen exercise/exam to answer questions on various social work case studies.'
>
> Jane Tope, Access to Caring Professions tutor

> 'It was the worst interview I've ever had – it was quite nerve racking. The time element as much as anything – I put my form in at the beginning of October and I didn't hear until early January that I had an interview on the 24th. It was an all day thing, I had to write an essay on a health related topic from a magazine and there was an interview after lunch with a qualified midwife and a lecturer.'
>
> Polly Stephen, Access student

Entering the interview room in a positive frame of mind is important. Immediately prior to your interview take a positive look at yourself, to assess your strengths, and to remind yourself why you would be a good person to be offered a university or college place.

When mature students are asked to name strengths that students coming directly from school may lack, the lists are usually very impressive. Mature applicants have a range of life skills related to independent living. They are accustomed to organising their lives, to working on their own initiative and, perhaps, not least, getting out of bed in the morning!

Likely questions:

> ?
>
> Why do you want to study for a degree/diploma now?
> Why do you want to study biology/dance – whatever
> else you have chosen?
> Why do you want to study at this particular
> institution?
> Tell me about your previous studying experiences?
> Tell me about a book you have read recently?
> Where else have you applied?

One fear that applicants have is not understanding the question. It's better to say 'I'm afraid I haven't been introduced to that topic' than to bluff your way through.

Have some questions ready for the end of the interview. Try to show that you are familiar with the course when you put your questions to the interviewer. Some useful examples are:

> ?
>
> What proportion of mature students were on the
> course in the past?
> How well have such students done?
> How is the course assessed?
> How are work placements organised?
> Is timetabling organised to fit in with the needs of
> student parents?
> What does a weekly timetable of a student on this
> course look like? How frequently does it change?

OFFERS FROM UCAS

Offers of places are sent to you via UCAS. You can hold two offers under the present UCAS system. There are three possibilities:

- **Unconditional offers** – this means that the institution is happy to admit you on the basis of what you currently have to offer
- **Conditional offers** – this means that the institution will accept you if you obtain certain qualifications e.g. successful completion of an access course
- **Insurance offers** – you can hold one other offer as insurance if you fail to meet the conditions of the conditional offer.

If you are not made an offer from any of the universities you have applied to, you can apply through a system called 'Extra' for other courses. This usually starts in the spring.

In August, a system called 'Clearing' operates where courses still requiring students are publicised, both in the national press and through UCAS. You can apply to courses that still have vacancies if you are not currently holding any other offers. UCAS advises mature students not to wait for Clearing but to contact institutions before then, as Clearing is geared largely towards standard entrants awaiting A-level results.

If you need to apply through Clearing, you should look at the lists and assess the available courses in the same way you did with your original choices, using the appropriate prospectuses. Once you have decided on a possible course, phone or visit the institution and have a chat with the admissions tutor. At this stage, all offers are informal and may only become a definite commitment once the official Clearing Entry Form is in the hands of the admissions tutor.

Try not to be panicked into accepting a place on what might turn out to be an unsuitable course; you may need to reassess what you should do at this stage. If you decide you need more help, see the *Introduction* for details of where you can get further advice.

CHAPTER SEVEN

CHECKLIST

By now you will have had the chance to investigate:

- what's on offer in HE
- what to expect from study
- practical issues applicable to you – finance, accommodation, childcare
- the effect on you and those close to you
- your reasons for studying
- career issues
- if you need further qualifications for entry to courses
- if you need any advance preparation for studying
- factors to consider when choosing a course and an institution
- details of how to apply.

This is the time to reflect and decide if you want to continue with the idea. Use this checklist to help weigh up the pros and cons:

Yes   No

Personal

☐ ☐ Will study help your personal aims?

☐ ☐ Is the size of the university right for you?

☐ ☐ Is the location of the university right for you?

☐ ☐ Do you feel comfortable with the atmosphere of the place?

Academic

☐ ☐ Is the course at the right level of study for you?

☐ ☐ Have you enough interest in the subjects to sustain you for the length of the course?

☐ ☐ How good are the study facilities e.g. computers, library facilities?

☐ ☐ Will you get the level of support you need?

Yes   No

Career

☐   ☐   Will study further your career aims – have you realistically assessed your chances of an appropriate job?

☐   ☐   Is the course recognised by the professional field you hope to enter?

☐   ☐   If you decide to study further, will the course lead onto a higher level course?

Practical

☐   ☐   Will the course fit with your personal circumstances e.g. hours of study?

☐   ☐   Is the course flexible enough for you – so you can change how you study if your circumstances change?

☐   ☐   Does the course offer a range of study methods to suit you e.g. online library access?

☐   ☐   Transport – are all parts of the course easily accessible – study on campus and any placements?

☐   ☐   Do you think you will be able to manage financially?

☐   ☐   Childcare – if needed, is it available, affordable and appropriate for the next few years?

☐   ☐   Accommodation – if you plan to move there, what will be on offer and is it affordable?

CHAPTER EIGHT

WHEN YOU GET THERE

THE FIRST FEW DAYS

Knowing what to expect when you get there can help with first day nerves. The first thing you need to do is enrol. Make sure you take all the relevant documents, plenty of passport-sized photographs and be prepared for a few queues.

The first few days can be a bit daunting, but remember that it will be the same for everyone. Comments from research in the London area, as part of a collaborative Widening Participation project, include:

> 'Finding your way around those first few days is difficult. Universities are considerably bigger than colleges or schools. Signposting and security make it daunting and some people reported missing out on vital bits of the programme or being late because they didn't know where to go.'
>
> (Student Voice March 2000 – Julia Dinsdale)

JOIN IN WITH WHAT'S ON OFFER

Mature students have other lives outside university, and it's easy to come to lectures and go home again. Those who do try and join in what's on offer appreciate the extra dimension:

> 'When I came here I didn't know anybody, so I joined the volleyball club to make sure I knew some people – I did this for the first two years. As you change modules you meet a new set of people – so you see the original people you met less, as each semester goes by. It would be easy to just come to lectures and go away again and not have anyone to talk to.'
>
> Jacci Qualters, English and Literary Studies and Media and Cultural Studies student

'My advice is: no matter how old you are, join in the "freshers" week' activities at the start of the year. Home in on the other mature students and talk to everyone you sit next to.' Kevin Boreham, Business Management student

SETTLING IN

Re-entering education is a major change for older students. Anxiety and lack of confidence are common feelings. Although many worry about fitting in with younger students, this is in reality rarely a problem and mixing with other students of all ages is very positive for all concerned. Your confidence develops and, as the college or university becomes more familiar and you make social contacts, you feel free to enjoy your new life.

'There aren't many mature students on my course but before I was offered a place I had an interview with two representatives from the business school who asked how I felt about that. It didn't bother me and I haven't had any problems – mixing with the younger students is fine. At the end of the day we are all studying the same thing.'

Robyn Budge, Commerce student

Virtually all mature students lack confidence in their academic ability and assume that the younger students will be more capable. Gradually, this assumption is replaced by the realisation that they have many advantages.

See Chapter Two *What to expect* for more ideas to help with settling in and the section on Personal needs in Chapter Six *Getting in – choosing a course and applying for a place.*

SUPPORT FOR MATURE STUDENTS

If you need extra help with settling in, there are people on campus who can help. Many universities have mature student officers. For details, see the university listings in this directory.

'A "mature student" is anyone over the age of 21 and as such, this is a diverse group of people, bringing with them their own uniqueness. It is important for mature students to be aware of the support that is available to them at university. We recognise that mature students'

personal, social, financial and educational circumstances may well differ considerably from those of younger students, and will give rise to different needs and requirements. It is the role of the student support and counselling service to listen to and respond to any such needs, and, if necessary, to provide an official channel of communication to the relevant committees and institutions of the university. At Birmingham we have a mature student population of approximately 10 per cent and recognise their support needs as being different and wide ranging, and of equal importance to those of the traditional 18–21-year-old students.'

Nahid Saiyed, Mature Students Co-ordinator,
Student Support and Counselling

Who can help?

Most universities and colleges will have:

Mature student officers	Specialist staff may be available in the admissions office of the university, or the students' union
Personal tutors	Your tutor is often the first point of contact when you need extra help. Some universities have welfare tutors to help with personal issues and academic tutors to help with academic issues and feedback on your progress
Counsellors	Trained counsellors are available in universities and colleges to give one-to-one help and run groups to deal with individual problems or areas like exam stress
Finance support officers	Most universities have a financial support office to advise students on funding and sources of help
Mature student mentors	Some universities e.g. University of Newcastle upon Tyne, run a scheme where second or third year mature students act as mentors to first year students
Learning support staff	Support for students who want to improve their skills such as essay writing or IT skills, is sometimes provided by a learning support team, who assess your needs and provide appropriate support

STUDENT FACILITIES AND SERVICES

On most campuses you will find not only academic amenities, such as libraries, workshops and computer clusters, but also a range of personal and support services, such as shops, catering, childcare facilities, accommodation, health centres, and sports, social, recreational and religious amenities. These are available to all students, whatever their age, and whether or not they live in university or college accommodation.

Students' unions

> *'Mature students sometimes do not use their students' union because they assume they are all about social events, but they have many services to offer, even if you just get your student discount card.'*
>
> *Julia Dinsdale, Community Liaison Officer*

At University College Worcester, research led to establishing a 'buddy scheme'. Pat Tromans, the Executive Officer on the Students' Union with a remit for mature students comments:

> *'Through the "buddy scheme", meetings are organised and publicised twice a month – at different times – lunch and early evening on different days to allow the chance for more people to attend. They are group sessions where students discuss any issues that are concerning them. Most issues we sort out among ourselves at the meetings, others I can take forward to the college via the students' union.'*

Amenities are often provided by, or with the assistance of the students' unions, which exist to represent students' interests at institutional and national level, as well as providing a variety of student-run services on the campus. They often help organise mature student societies, and may appoint officers to represent the special interests of mature students on their organising committees. For details, see the university listings in this directory.

All students automatically become members of the students' union when they enrol. The National Union of Students has an informative website (www.nusonline.co.uk) and there is also a national Mature Students Union (MSU) website (www.msu.org.uk).

CHAPTER NINE

FURTHER INFORMATION

BOOKS AND OTHER RESOURCES

Access to Higher Education Course Directory 2001, Leeds Metropolitan University

Bridging the Gap, A Guide to Disabled Students' Allowances in Higher Education, DfES Annual

The Careers Guide, Penguin

Childcare Grant and Other Financial Help for Student Parents in Higher Edcation, DfES Annual

Degree Course Offers, B. Heap, Trotman Annual

Directory of Grant-making Trusts, Charities Aid Foundation

Directory of Guidance Provsion for Adults in the UK, ADSET

The Disabled Students' Guide to University, Trotman Annual

Educational Grants Directory, Directory of Social Change

Exams Without Anxiety, David Acres, Deanhouse

Financial Assistance for Students with Disabilities in Higher Education, Skill

Financial Support for Higher Education Students 2003/2004, DfES (for people living in England and Wales)

Financial Support for Students: A Guide to Grants, Loans and Fees in Higher Education, Department of Education (for people living in Northern Ireland)

The Good Study Guide, Andy Northedge, Open University Press

The Grants Register, Macmillan

Guide to Higher Education for People with Disabilities, UCAS and Skill

Guide to Students' Allowances, SAAS (for people living in Scotland)

How I got my First Class Degree, P. Tolmie, IHE Series, 1998

How to Complete your UCAS Form, Trotman

Learner's Guide, Open University, www.open.ac.uk

Mature Students' Guide to Higher Education, UCAS Annual

Moving Forward, Leicestershire Learning and Skills Council 2003

Moving On, Dr Jill Terry, Collaborative Widening Participation Project

(Coventry University, University College Worcester, the University of Warwick) 024 7688 7109 www.coventry.ac.uk (search for 'widening participation')

Occupations, Connexions, Annual

Second Chances, Eileen D'Ath, Tessa Doe, Helen Evans, Debbie Steel, Lifetime Careers 2002

The Student Book, Boehm and Lees-Spalding, Trotman 2003

The Students' Guide to Writing Essays, D. Roberts, Kogan Page 1999

Students' Support Sponsorship Funding Directory, CRAC/Hobsons

Students' Money Matters, Gwenda Thomas, Trotman 2003

Study Skills Handbook, S. Cotrell, Palgrave 1999

UCAS/Universities Scotland Entrance Guide to Higher Education in Scotland 2004, UCAS Universities Scotland

University & College Entrance, UCAS (details entry requirements for all courses)

University Scholarships & Awards, Brian Heap, Trotman

Research

Research referred to in the text:

Educating Rita and Her Sisters, Benn, R., Elliott, J. and Whaley, P. (eds) (1998) NIACE

Ethnic Choosing: Minority Ethnic Students, Social Class and Higher Education Choice, Ball S.J., Reay D., David M. (2002)

Student and Community Voice – Working on Widening Participation Issue 3, Collaborative Widening Participation project (City University, University of East London, London Guildhall University, University of North London, Open University in London, Queen Mary University of London) (July 2001)

USEFUL CONTACTS AND WEBSITES

Access courses database – lists accredited Access courses nationally – www.ucas.com/access

Age Positive – government website to raise awareness of the advantages of employing older people – www.agepositive.gov.uk

Association of Graduate Careers Advisory Services – university careers centres throughout the country – some will give advice to you before you apply for a course, for others you have to be a registered student – www.agcas.org.uk

Career development loans – details on loans for some vocational courses
– www.lifelonglearning.dfes.gov.uk/cdl (Tel: 0800 585 505)

Careers Scotland – provides careers information, advice and guidance to
Scots of all ages – www.careers-scotland.org.uk (Tel: 0845 8502 502)

Careers Wales – all age careers information, advice and guidance services
– www.careerswales.com

Childcare Link – lists childcare facilities available by area –
www.childcarelink.gov.uk (Tel: 08000 960296)

Connexions – careers advice and guidance in England –
www.connexions.gov.uk

Dance and Drama – Department for Education and Skills details on
awards for dance and drama students – www.dfes.gov.uk/dancedrama

Department for Education and Skills – information on student finance –
www.dfes.gov.uk/studentsupport (Information line tel: 0800 731 9133)

Department of Health – www.doh.gov.uk/hcsmain.htm – Information
about NHS bursaries to study health related courses e.g. nursing –
England – The NHS Student Grants Unit, Room 212C, Government
Buildings, Norcross, Blackpool FY5 3TA (Tel: 01253 332627). **Wales** –
Student Awards Unit, NHS Human Resources Division, National
Assembly for Wales, Cathays Park, Cardiff CF10 3NQ (Tel: 029
20826893). **Scotland** – Student Awards Agency for Scotland, 3
Redheughs Rigg, South Gyle, Edinburgh EH12 9YT (Tel: 0845 111
1711). **Northern Ireland** – The Department of Health, Social Services
and Public Safety, Human Resources Directorate, Workforce
Development Unit, Room 3B, Dundonald House, Upper Newtownards,
Belfast BT4 3SF.

**Department of Higher and Further Education Training and
Employment** – information on financial support for students living in
Northern Ireland – Rathgael House, Balloo Road, Bangor, Co Down
BT19 7PR – www.deni.gov.uk (Tel: 02891 279279)

Department of Work and Pensions – information on jobcentres and the
former Social Security offices and Benefits Agency www.dwp.gov.uk

Disability Rights Commission – information on Disability Discrimination
Act – www.drc-gb.org (Tel 08457 622 633)

Distance Learning – www.distance-learning.hobsons.com

Doctor Job – careers website for graduates www.doctorjob.com

Edexcel Foundation – examining body – www.edexcel.org.uk (Tel: 0870
240 9800)

Educational Grants Advisory Service (EGAS) – provides independent advice on funding for further and higher education 501–505 Kingsland Road, Dalston, London E8 4AU (Tel: 020 7249 6636) www.egas-online.org.uk

Employers Forum on Age – discussion group with up to date information – www.efa.org.uk

Foundation Degrees – information on the new two year foundation degrees – www.foundationdegree.org.uk

Guidance Council – for help with finding local information, advice and guidance (IAG) providers – www.guidancecouncil.com

Hero – includes links to university prospectuses, information on choosing a course and funding etc – www.hero.ac.uk

Homestudy – information on distance learning courses – www.homestudy.org.uk

Inland Revenue – information on child tax credits and working tax credits www.inlandrevenue.gov.uk/taxcredits (Tel: 0845 300 3900)

Jobcentre Plus – information on benefit entitlements and access to jobs. Includes former Social Security offices and Benefits Agency in addition to jobcentre services – www.jobcentreplus.gov.uk

Learndirect – government information site about courses on offer nationwide – www.learndirect.co.uk – also runs some courses online and gives information on university courses under the 'Learning Through Work' scheme – www.learndirect.ltw.co.uk

Learning and Skills Council (LSC) – will provide information on local LSC organisations – www.lsc.gov.uk

Lifelong Learning – part of DfES website www.lifelonglearning.co.uk

Mature Student Union (MSU) – national student union for mature students – www.msu.org.uk

National Institute of Adult Continuing Education (NIACE) – promotes the study and advancement of adult education – www.niace.org.uk

National Association for Education Guidance for Adults (NAEGA) – links to local networks for educational guidance for adults – www.naega.org.uk

National Extension College – offers courses through distance learning – Michael Young Centre, Purbeck Road, Cambridge CB2 2HN (Tel: 01223 450200) – www.nec.ac.uk

National Union of Students (NUS) – www.nusonline.co.uk

Northern Ireland Careers Service – based in jobcentres and jobs and benefits offices. Careers Officers provide impartial information and guidance service – www.delni.gov.uk (Tel: 0800 353530)

Open University Students' Enquiry Service – for degree course programmes by distance learning and access to study skills materials. PO Box 200, Milton Keynes MK7 6AA – www.open.ac.uk (Tel: 01908 653231)

Prospects – national graduate careers information and jobs – www.prospects.ac.uk

Qualifications and Curriculum Authority – for information on current qualifications and the national qualifications framework – www.qca.org.uk

Scottish Credit and Qualification Framework – www.scqf.org.uk

Scottish Wider Access Programme – information on access courses – www.swap2highereducation.com

Skill – organisation for students with disabilities – Chapter House, 18–20 Crucifix Lane, London SE1 3JW – www.skill.org.uk (Tel: 0800 3285050)

Skills4study – website includes advice on study skills – www.skills4study.com

Student Awards Agency for Scotland – information on financial support for students living in Scotland – 3 Redheughs Rigg, South Gyle, Edinburgh EH12 9YT. Tel: 0845 111 1711 – www.saas.gov.uk

Student Loans Company – 100 Bothwell Street, Glasgow G2 7JD – www.slc.co.uk (Tel: 0800 405010)

Student UK – website includes financial advice for students – www.studentuk.com

Support4learning – includes information on financing your studies – www.support4learning.org.uk

Trotman Publishing – 2 The Green, Richmond, Surrey TW9 1PL – www.careers-portal.co.uk (Tel: 020 8486 1150)

UCAS – Universities and Colleges Admissions Service – Rosehill, New Barn Lane, Cheltenham, Gloucestershire GL52 3LZ – www.ucas.com, Helpline tel: 0242 227788/0870 1122211

UK Qualifications – www.ucas.com/candq/ukquals/index.html

Uni4me – website with details for mature students – www.uni4me.com

University of the Third Age – promotes lifelong learning among older people – 26 Harrison Street, London WC1H 8JG – www.u3a.org.uk (Tel: 020 7837 8838)

Welsh National Assembly Learning Grant – Tel: 02920 825 831

Workers' Educational Association – runs adult courses – Temple House, 17 Victoria Park Square, London E2 9PB – www.wea.org.uk (Tel: 020 8983 1515)

INSTITUTIONS

University of Aberdeen
King's College
Aberdeen
AB24 3FX
Phone: 01224 272000
Email: sras@abdn.ac.uk
Website: www.abdn.ac.uk
Total number of students at institution: 13,000
Total number of mature students: 19 per cent of undergraduates.

Student Recruitment and Admissions Service
Phone: 01224 272090/1
Fax: 01224 272576
Email: sras@abdn.ac.uk

Applications
General entry qualifications that are considered acceptable for mature
applicants without the normal standard entry qualifications:

Access Course	Yes
Essay submission	No
Entrance exam	No
APEL/APL	Yes
Other	All applicants are considered on a case by case basis.

The institution does not interview all mature applicants.

Funding
There are no specific mature student bursaries available over and above the
national funds.

Study
Negotiated flexible learning is not available on all courses.
It is available to:

Full-time students	No
Part-time students	Yes
Distance Learning students	Yes

Timetabling hours

Lectures are timetabled between 9am and 6pm.

Some modules can be studied that require attending only morning lectures, depending on subject and courses chosen.

Accommodation and childcare

Accommodation is available:

Specifically for mature students	No – however, accommodation is guaranteed to all new students.
For mature students with families	Yes – it is possible to arrange to rent a flat or house through the University.

The institution does have crèche/childcare facilities.
Spaces are always available.

General

There are societies or organised social activities for mature students.

There is online information specifically for mature students, and www.abdn.ac.uk/sras gives admissions information for all students, including mature students.

The Key Learning Opportunities Unit works with students who don't have the standard entry requirements.

University of Abertay Dundee

Bell Street
Dundee
DD1 1HG
Contact: Julie McEwan
Phone: 01382 308080
Fax: 01382 308081
Email: sro@abertay.ac.uk
Website: www.abertay.ac.uk

Total number of students at institution: 4,700
Total number of mature students: 2,000

Student Support Officer

Phone: 01382 308051
Email: studentservices@abertay.ac.uk

Applications

General entry qualifications that are considered acceptable for mature
applicants without the normal standard entry qualifications:

Access Course	Yes
Essay submission	Yes
Entrance exam	No
APEL/APL	Yes
Other	FE qualifications

The institution does not interview all mature applicants.

Funding

There are no specific mature student bursaries available over and above the
national funds.

Study

Negotiated flexible learning is not available on most courses.

Timetabling hours

Lectures are timetabled between 9am and 6pm.
Modules can be studied that require attending only morning lectures.

Accommodation and childcare

Accommodation is available:

Specifically for mature students	Yes
For mature students with families	No

The institution does not have crèche/childcare facilities.

General

There are no societies or organised social activities for mature students at
present, but students are allowed to set up their own society through the
students' association.

Information on entry requirements for mature applicants is available online.

College of Agriculture, Food and Rural Enterprise

Greenmount Campus
22 Greenmount Road
Antrim
Co. Antrim
BT41 4PU
Phone: 028 9442 6700
Fax: 028 9442 6606
Website: www.cafre.ac.uk
Total number of students at institution: 1,400
Total number of mature students: 200

Applications

General entry qualifications that are considered acceptable for mature applicants without the normal standard entry qualifications:

Access Course	Yes
APEL/APL	Yes
Other	Industry experience.

The institution does not interview all mature applicants.

Funding

There are no specific mature student bursaries available over and above the national funds.

Study

Negotiated flexible learning is available on some courses, but only to part-time students.

Timetabling hours

Lectures are timetabled between 9.15am and 4.45pm.
Occasionally, modules can be studied that require attending only morning lectures.

Accommodation and childcare
Accommodation is available:

Specifically for mature students	No – but self-catering en-suite accommodation is available.
For mature students with families	No

The institution does not have crèche/childcare facilities.

General
There are no societies or organised social activities for mature students. The institution says it will discuss needs and requirements on an individual basis with each student and will endeavour to meet these as far as possible.

ALRA (Academy of Live and Recorded Arts)
Royal Patriotic Building
Fitzhugh Grove
Trinity Road
London
SW18 3SX
Phone: 020 8870 6475
Fax: 020 8875 0789
Email: lee@alra.demon.co.uk
Website: www.alra.demon.co.uk
Total number of students at institution: 120
Total number of mature students: c. 30

Student Support Officer
Lee McOwan
Phone: 020 8870 6475
Fax: 020 8875 0789
Email: lee@alra.demon.co.uk

Applications
General entry qualifications that are considered acceptable for mature applicants without the normal standard entry qualifications:

Other	Audition/interview

The institution does interview all mature applicants.

Funding

There are no specific mature student bursaries available over and above the national funds.

Study

Negotiated flexible learning is not available on most courses.

Timetabling hours

Lectures are timetabled between 9am and 6pm.

Modules cannot be studied that require attending only morning lectures.

Accommodation and childcare

Accommodation is available:

Specifically for mature students	No
For mature students with families	No

The institution does not have crèche/childcare facilities.

General

There are no societies or organised social activities for mature students.

There is no online information specifically for mature students.

The institution welcomes mature students, particularly on its one-year acting course.

Anglia Polytechnic University

East Road

Cambridge

CB4 1BX

Phone: 01223 363271

Fax: 01223 417719

Email: cam@apu.ac.uk

Website: www.apu.ac.uk

Total number of students at institution: 25,627

Career Service
Email: careers-cam@apu.ac.uk

Applications
General entry qualifications that are considered acceptable for mature applicants without the normal standard entry qualifications:

Access Course	Yes
Essay submission	Yes
APEL/APL	Yes

The institution does not interview all mature applicants.

Funding
There are no specific mature student bursaries available over and above the national funds.

Study
Negotiated flexible learning is available on most courses.
It is available to:

Full-time students	Yes
Part-time students	Yes
Distance Learning students	No

Timetabling hours
Lectures are timetabled between 9am and 6pm.
Modules cannot be studied that require attending only morning lectures.

Accommodation and childcare
Accommodation is available:

Specifically for mature students	No
For mature students with families	No

The institution does have crèche/childcare facilities.
There are 50 spaces.
Spaces are not always available.

General
The mature students' society organises social activities for mature students.

There is online information specifically for mature students:
www.apu.ac.uk/careers – follow route to Mature Student Guide

Arts Institute at Bournemouth
Wallisdown
Poole
Dorset
BH12 5HH
Phone: 01202 533011
Fax: 01202 537729
Email: general@aib.ac.uk
Website: www.aib.ac.uk
Total number of students at institution: 1,012
Total number of mature students: 524

Student Advice Centre
Phone: 01202 363220
Email: studentadvice@aib.ac.uk

Applications
General entry qualifications that are considered acceptable for mature
applicants without the normal standard entry qualifications:

Access Course	Yes
Essay submission	No
Entrance exam	No
APEL/APL	Yes

The institution does interview all mature applicants.

Funding
There are no specific mature student bursaries available over and above the
national funds.

Study
Negotiated flexible learning is available on most courses.
It is available to:

Full-time students	Yes
Part-time students	Yes
Distance Learning students	No

Timetabling hours

Lectures are timetabled between 8.30am and 9pm.
Modules cannot be studied that require attending only morning lectures.

Accommodation and childcare

Accommodation is available:

Specifically for mature students	No
For mature students with families	No

The institution does not have crèche/childcare facilities.
Financial help with childcare is available through the Student Advice Centre.

General

There are no societies or organised social activities for mature students.
There is no online information specifically for mature students.

Askham Bryan College

Askham Bryan
York
YO23 3FR
Phone: 01904 772277
Fax: 01904 772288
Website: www.askham-bryan.ac.uk
Total number of students at institution: 500
Total number of mature students: 100

Student Support Officer

Jill Ellis
Phone: 01904 772222
Fax: 01904 772288
Email: je@askham-bryan.ac.uk

Applications

General entry qualifications that are considered acceptable for mature applicants without the normal standard entry qualifications:

Access Course	Yes
Essay submission	No
Entrance exam	No
APEL/APL	Yes

The institution does not interview all mature applicants.

Funding

There are no specific mature student bursaries available over and above the national funds.

Study

Negotiated flexible learning is available on most courses.
It is available to:

Full-time students	Yes
Part-time students	Yes

Timetabling hours

Lectures are timetabled between 9.00am and 5.30pm.
Modules cannot be studied that require attending only morning lectures.

Accommodation and childcare

Accommodation is available:

Specifically for mature students	No
For mature students with families	No

The institution does have crèche/childcare facilities.
Spaces are not always available.

General

There are no societies or organised social activities for mature students.

Aylesbury College
Oxford Road
Aylesbury
Buckinghamshire
HP21 8PD
Phone: 01296 588588
Fax: 01296 588589
Website: www.aylesbury.ac.uk

Student Support Officer
Maggi Campbell Keith
Phone: 01296 588591
Fax: 01296 588591
Email: mcampbell@aylesbury.ac.uk

Applications
The institution does not interview all mature applicants.

Funding
There are no specific mature student bursaries available over and above the national funds.

Study
Negotiated flexible learning is not available on most courses.

Timetabling hours
Lectures are timetabled between 9am and 9pm.

Accommodation and childcare
Accommodation is available:

Specifically for mature students	No
For mature students with families	No

The institution does have crèche/childcare facilities.
Spaces are not always available.
Other local childcare is available.

General
There are no societies or organised social activities for mature students.

Barking College

Dagenham Road
Romford
Essex
RM7 0XU
Phone: 01708 770000
Fax: 01708 770007
Email: admissions@barkingcollege.ac.uk
Website: www.barkingcollege.ac.uk`
Total number of students at institution: c. 12,000
Total number of mature students: c. 8,000

Student Support Officer

Sue Kemmis, College Counsellor

Applications

General entry qualifications that are considered acceptable for mature
applicants without the normal standard entry qualifications:

Access Course	Yes
Essay submission	Yes
Entrance exam	Yes
APEL/APL	Yes

The institution does not interview all mature applicants.

Funding

There are specific mature student bursaries available over and above the
national funds.

Study

Negotiated flexible learning is not available on most courses.

Timetabling hours

Lectures are timetabled between 9am and 9pm.
Modules cannot be studied that require attending only morning lectures.

Accommodation and childcare

Accommodation is available:

Specifically for mature students	No
For mature students with families	No

The institution does have crèche/childcare facilities.
There are 14 spaces.
Spaces are not always available.

General
There are no societies or organised social activities for mature students.

Barnet College
Wood Street Centre
High Barnet
EN5 4AZ
Phone: 020 8440 6321
Fax: 020 8441 5236
Email: info@barnet.ac.uk
Website: www.barnet.ac.uk
Total number of students at institution: 25,000

Student Support Officer
Phone: 020 8275 2856

Applications
All full-programme applicants are interviewed for their course. See individual course details in the prospectus for specific admissions requirements.

Funding
There are no specific mature student bursaries available over and above the national funds.

Study
For information regarding negotiated flexible learning please contact admissions.

Timetabling hours
Modules can be studied that require attending only morning lectures.

Accommodation and childcare

Accommodation is available:

Specifically for mature students	No
For mature students with families	No

The institution does have crèche/childcare facilities.
Spaces are limited.
For further information call 020 8226 4029 (Grahame Park Centre) or
020 8362 8024 (Russell Lane Centre).

Barnfield College

Enterprise Way
Luton
Bedfordshire
LU3 4BU
Phone: 01582 569500
Website: www.barnfield.ac.uk

Applications

General entry qualifications that are considered acceptable for mature
applicants without the normal standard entry qualifications vary from
course to course.
The institution does interview all mature applicants for full-time courses
but not for part-time courses.

Funding

There are specific mature student bursaries available over and above the
national funds. There is normal Learner Support Funds, assistance and this
is an Adult Learning Grant pilot area.

Study

Negotiated flexible learning is not available on most courses.

Timetabling hours

Lectures are usually timetabled between 9am and 9.30pm, but this can
vary.
Modules cannot be studied that require attending only morning
lectures/lessons.

Accommodation and childcare

Accommodation is available:

Specifically for mature students	No
For mature students with families	No

The institution does have crèche/childcare facilities.
There are 52 spaces.
Spaces are always available.
The facility operates on a 'first come, first served' basis.

General

There are no societies or organised social activities for mature students.

Bath Spa University College

Newton Park
Newton St Loe
Bath
BA2 9BN
Phone: 01225 875875
Fax: 01225 875444
Email: enquiries@bathspa.ac.uk
Website: www.bathspa.ac.uk
Total number of students at institution: 4,500
Total number of mature students: 1,485 (33 per cent) of students are over
21; 1125 (25 per cent) are over 25.

Centre for Development and Participation

Phone: 01225 875796
Fax: 01225 876241
Email: j.jancovich@bathspa.ac.uk

Applications

General entry qualifications that are considered acceptable for mature
applicants without the normal standard entry qualifications:

Access Course	Yes – conditional offers are made on the basis of Access Course.
Essay submission	Yes – for some subjects.
Entrance exam	No
APEL/APL	Yes
Other	Audition/portfolio for Fine Art/ Performance Art/ Music

The institution does not interview all mature applicants.

Funding
There are no specific mature student bursaries available over and above the national funds.

Study
Negotiated flexible learning is available on some courses.
It is available to:

Full-time students	No
Part-time students	Yes – all courses are available on a part-time basis.
Other	Online learning is available.

Timetabling hours
Lectures are timetabled between 9am and 6pm.
Modules can be studied that require attending only morning lectures.

Accommodation and childcare
Accommodation is available:

Specifically for mature students	No – however, the institution tries to accommodate all first-year students on campus.
For mature students with families	No

The institution does have crèche/childcare facilities.
Spaces are not always available.
The nursery is for children aged 0–5 and is divided into three areas: 0–2, 2–3, and 3–5.

General
There is a Mature Students Society, and other societies vary from year to year.
Bath Spa has dedicated open days for mature students. There is a conference in January for Access students, and a summer school for mature students in September. There is a 'buddying' system scheme, which partners new mature students with a mature student already at the institution.

Birkbeck, University of London
Malet Street
Bloomsbury
London
WC1E 7HX
Phone: 020 7631 6000
Fax: 020 7631 6270
Website: www.bbk.ac.uk
Total number of mature students at institution: undergraduate 3,941; postgraduate 3,272; continuing education 8,467

Applications
General entry qualifications that are considered acceptable for mature applicants without the normal standard entry qualifications:

Other	Flexible entry, no formal qualifications for undergraduate students.

The institution does not interview all mature applicants.

Funding

There are no specific mature student bursaries available over and above the national funds.

Study

Negotiated flexible learning is not available on most courses.
Undergraduate courses are all taught part-time in the evening over four years.

Timetabling hours

Lectures are timetabled between 6pm and 9pm.
Modules cannot be studied that require attending only morning lectures.

Accommodation and childcare

Accommodation is available:

Specifically for mature students	No
For mature students with families	No

The institution does have crèche/childcare facilities.
There are 12 spaces.
Spaces are not always available.

General

There are societies or organised social activities for mature students.

University of Birmingham

Edgbaston
Birmingham
B15 2TT
Phone: 0121 414 3344
Website: www.bham.ac.uk

Total number of students at institution: 27,048
Total number of mature students: 9,967

Student Support Officer

Nahid Saiyed
Phone: 0121 414 2741
Email: N.Saiyed@bham.ac.uk

Applications

General entry qualifications that are considered acceptable for mature
applicants without the normal standard entry qualifications:

Access Course	Yes
APEL/APL	Yes

The institution does not interview all mature applicants.
For further advice on the suitability of your qualifications and experience,
contact the relevant school or department direct. There is a mature
students' entry scheme for students on Access to Higher Education
programmes. Contact Dr David Whitston for further information by email
(K.Whitston@bham.ac.uk) or telephone 0121 414 7169.

Funding

There are no specific mature student bursaries available over and above the
national funds.

Study

Contact the relevant school or department for advice on the availability of
negotiated flexible learning.

Timetabling hours

Generally, lectures are timetabled between 9am and 6pm.
Contact the relevant school or department about the possibility of modules
being studied that require attending only morning lectures.

Accommodation and childcare

Accommodation is available:

Specifically for mature students	No
For mature students with families	Yes – call 0121 414 6438 for information.

The institution does have crèche/childcare facilities.
Spaces are not always available.

General

There are societies for mature students: the Mature Students' Committee;
the Postgraduate Committee; and the Mature and Postgraduate Students'
Association.

Contact the Guild of Students for more information:
email pso@bugs.bham.ac.uk; telephone 0121 472 1841;
website www.bugs.bham.ac.uk

There is online information specifically for mature students at
www.undergraduate.bham.ac.uk/mature.htm

Advice and Representation Centre (ARC)
Phone: 0121 427 1841 ext. 2259
Email: welfare@guild.bham.ac.uk
Website: www.bugs.bham.ac.uk/support/arc/home.asp

Centre for Lifelong Learning
Phone: 0121 414 3413
Website: www.cll.bham.ac.uk

Financial Support Office
Phone: 0121 414 7391
Website: www.studserv.bham.ac.uk/fsoffice/

Student Support and Counselling Service
Phone: 0121 414 5130
Website:www.sscs.bham.ac.uk

Widening Participation Unit
Phone: 0121 414 7169
Website: www.marketing.bham.ac.uk/wideningparticipation

Bishop Burton College

Bishop Burton
Beverley
East Yorkshire
HU17 8QG
Phone: 01964 553000
Fax: 01964 553101
Email: enquiries@bishopburton.ac.uk
Website: www.bishopburton.ac.uk

Student Support Officer

Carole Allchorne
Phone: 01964 553000
Fax: 01964 553101

Applications

General entry qualifications that are considered acceptable for mature applicants without the normal standard entry qualifications:

Access Course	Yes
Essay submission	No
Entrance exam	No
APEL/APL	Yes
Other	Life experience

The institution does not interview all mature applicants.

Funding

There are no specific mature student bursaries available over and above the national funds.

Study

Negotiated flexible learning is not available on most courses.

Timetabling hours

Lectures are timetabled between 9am and 5pm.
Modules cannot be studied that require attending only morning lectures.

Accommodation and childcare

Accommodation is available:

Specifically for mature students	Yes
For mature students with families	No

The institution does not have crèche/childcare facilities, but this facility is being planned for the future.

General

There are societies or organised social activities for mature students.
There is no online information specifically for mature students.
The college specialises in providing education and training for mature students.

Bishop Grosseteste College

Lincoln
LN1 3DY
Phone: 01522 527347
Fax: 01522 530243
Email: registry@bgc.ac.uk
Website: www.bgc.ac.uk
Total number of students at institution: 953
Total number of mature students: 286

Mature Students' Officer

Claire Cook
Phone: 01522 527347
Email: claire.cook@bgc.ac.uk

Applications

General entry qualifications that are considered acceptable for mature applicants without the normal standard entry qualifications:

Access Course	Yes
Essay submission	Yes
Entrance exam	No
APEL/APL	Yes

The institution does interview all mature applicants.

Funding

There are no specific mature student bursaries available over and above the national funds.

Study

Negotiated flexible learning is not available on most courses.

Timetabling hours

Lectures are timetabled between 9.15am and 4.30pm.
Modules cannot be studied that require attending only morning lectures.

Accommodation and childcare

Accommodation is available:

Specifically for mature students	Yes – there is a semi-detached house 200 yards from the main campus designated for mature students.
For mature students with families	No – but the accommodation officer will assist all students in finding appropriate local accommodation.

The institution does not have crèche/childcare facilities.

General

There are societies or organised social activities for mature students, such as some family events.
There is online information specifically for mature students, such as some mature student profiles.
Bishop Grosseteste College prides itself on its strong tradition of welcoming mature students. For an informal chat, please contact Claire Cook.

Blackburn College
Feilden Street
Blackburn
BB2 1LH
Phone: 01254 55144
Fax: 01254 263947
Email: studentservices@blackburn.ac.uk
Website: www.blackburn.ac.uk
Total number of HE students at institution: 2,000
Total number of HE mature students: 1,400+

HE Marketing Officer
Pauline Shaw
Phone: 01254 292594
Email: p.shaw@blackburn.ac.uk

Applications
General entry qualifications that are considered acceptable for mature
applicants without the normal standard entry qualifications:

Access Course	Yes
Essay submission	No
Entrance exam	No
APEL/APL	Yes
Other	'Bridging' courses, aptitude test for BSc Computing.

The institution does interview all mature applicants.

Funding
There are no specific mature student bursaries available over and above the
national funds.

Study
Negotiated flexible learning is available on most courses.
It is available to:

Full-time students	Yes
Part-time students	Yes
Distance Learning students	Yes

Timetabling hours

Lectures are timetabled between 10am and 3pm.

Modules can be studied that require attending only morning lectures.

Accommodation and childcare

Accommodation is available:

Specifically for mature students	No
For mature students with families	No

The institution does have crèche/childcare facilities.

There are 110 spaces.

Spaces are not always available.

The crèche takes children up to the age of 5 and priority is given to full-time students.

General

There are no societies or organised social activities for mature students.

Blackfriars Hall and Studium

St Giles
Oxford
OX1 3LY
Phone: 01865 278441
Fax: 01865 278441
Email: secretary@blackfriars.ox.ac.uk
Website: www.bfriars.ox.ac.uk

Mature Students' Officer

Contact Hall Secretary

Student Support Officer

Contact Hall Secretary

Applications

General entry qualifications that are considered acceptable for mature applicants without the normal standard entry qualifications:

Essay submission	Yes

The institution does not interview all mature applicants.

Funding
There are no specific mature student bursaries available over and above the national funds.

Study
Negotiated flexible learning is not available on most courses.

Timetabling hours
Lectures are timetabled between 9am and 3pm.
Modules can be studied that require attending only morning lectures.

Accommodation and childcare
Accommodation is available:

Specifically for mature students	No
For mature students with families	No

The institution does not have crèche/childcare facilities.

General
Only accepts mature students in the relevant disciplines.

Blackpool and the Fylde College
Ashfield Road
Bispham
Blackpool
Lancashire
FY2 0HB
Phone: 01253 352352
Fax: 01253 356127
Email: visitors@blackpool.ac.uk
Website: www.blackpool.ac.uk
Total number of students at institution: 36,795

Student Support Officer
Phone: 01253 504351
Fax: 01253 356127

Applications

General entry qualifications that are considered acceptable for mature applicants without the normal standard entry qualifications:

Access Course	Yes
Essay submission	No
Entrance exam	No
APEL/APL	Yes
Other	Interview

The institution does interview all mature applicants.

Funding

There are specific mature student bursaries available over and above the national funds.

Study

Negotiated flexible learning is available on some courses.
It is available to:

Full-time students	No
Part-time students	Yes
Distance Learning students	Yes

Timetabling hours

Lectures are timetabled between 9am and 9pm.
Modules can be studied that require attending only morning lectures.

Accommodation and childcare

Accommodation is available:

Specifically for mature students	No
For mature students with families	No

The institution does have crèche/childcare facilities.
There are 20–24 spaces.
Spaces are always available.
There are nurseries on two campuses.

General

There are no societies or organised social activities for mature students.

Bolton Institute
Deane Road
Bolton
BL3 5AB
Phone: 01204 903903
Fax: 01204 903809
Email: enquiries@bolton.ac.uk
Website: www.bolton.ac.uk
Total number of students at institution: 7000
Total number of mature students: 2389 undergraduates

Student Information Service
Phone: 01204 903733
Fax: 01204 903732
Email: student-info-centre@bolton.ac.uk

Applications
General entry qualifications that are considered acceptable for mature
applicants without the normal standard entry qualifications:

Access Course	Yes
Essay submission	Yes
Entrance exam	Yes
APEL/APL	Yes

The institution does not interview all mature applicants.

Funding
There are no specific mature student bursaries available over and above the
national funds.

Study
Negotiated flexible learning is available on some courses.
It is available to:

Full-time students	Yes
Part-time students	Yes
Distance Learning students	Yes

Timetabling hours
Modules can be studied that require attending only morning lectures.

Accommodation and childcare
Accommodation is available:

Specifically for mature students	No
For mature students with families	No

The institution does not have crèche/childcare facilities.
Income for childcare is assessed, however.

General
There are no societies or organised social activities for mature students.
Mature applicants are welcomed.

Bournemouth University
Fern Barrow
Poole
Dorset
BH12 5BB
Phone: 01202 524111
Fax: 01202 702736
Email: marketing@bournemouth.ac.uk
Website: www.bournemouth.ac.uk
Total number of students at institution: 14,414
Total number of mature students: 9,643

Student Advice Centre
Phone: 01202 595779
Fax: 01202 535990
Email: studentadvice@bournemouth.ac.uk

Applications
General entry qualifications that are considered acceptable for mature
applicants without the normal standard entry qualifications:

Access Course	Yes
Essay submission	No
Entrance exam	No
APEL/APL	Yes

The institution does not interview all mature applicants.

Funding

There are no specific mature student bursaries available over and above the national funds.

Study

Negotiated flexible learning is available on some courses.
It is available to:

Full-time students	Yes
Part-time students	Yes
Distance Learning students	Yes

Timetabling hours

Lectures are timetabled between 9am and 9pm.
Modules can be studied that require attending only morning lectures.

Accommodation and childcare

Accommodation is available:

Specifically for mature students	No – all undergraduates, whether mature or not, can stay in university accommodation in the first year.
For mature students with families	No – but the accommodation service can help with finding rented accommodation.

The institution does have crèche/childcare facilities. Spaces are not always available but students have priority for places.

General

There are no societies or organised social activities for mature students. However, the Students' Union will support those wishing to run such a society.

There is online information specifically for mature students at www.bournemouth.ac.uk/new-students/mature-students.html

---

Bournemouth and Poole College

North Road
Parkstone
Poole
Dorset
BH14 0LS
Phone: 01202 747600
Fax: 01202 205601
Email: enquiries@thecollege.co.uk
Website: www.thecollege.co.uk

Mature Students' Officer

Phone: 01202 205612/205896
Email: adamsr@bpc.ac.uk

Applications

General entry qualifications that are considered acceptable for mature applicants without the normal standard entry qualifications:

Access Course	Yes
Essay submission	Yes
Entrance exam	Yes
APEL/APL	Yes

The institution does not interview all mature applicants.

Funding

There are no specific mature student bursaries available over and above the national funds.

Study

Negotiated flexible learning is available on some courses.
It is available to:

Full-time students	Not at present, but possibly.
Part-time students	Not at present, but possibly.
Distance Learning students	Yes

Timetabling hours

Lectures are timetabled between 9am and 9pm.
Modules can be studied that require attending only morning lectures.

Accommodation and childcare

Accommodation is available:

Specifically for mature students	No
For mature students with families	No

The institution does have crèche/childcare facilities.
There are 64 spaces.
Spaces are always available.
The baby unit caters for children aged 8 weeks to 5 years. It is generally open from 8am to 6pm in term-time (unless arranged otherwise).

General

There is a Mature Student Club.

University of Bradford

Richmond Road
Bradford
BD7 1DP
Phone: 01274 233081
Fax: 01274 236260
Email: course-enquiries@bradford.ac.uk
Website: www.bradford.ac.uk
Total number of students at institution: 9,742
Total number of mature students: 3,342 (34.3 per cent)

Mature Students' Officer
Phone: 01274 236235
Fax: 01274 236260
Email: p.k.gattaura@bradford.ac.uk

Applications
General entry qualifications that are considered acceptable for mature applicants without the normal standard entry qualifications:

Access Course	Yes
Essay submission	No
Entrance exam	No
APEL/APL	Yes

The institution does not interview all mature applicants.

Funding
There are no specific mature student bursaries available over and above the national funds.

Study
Negotiated flexible learning is not available on most courses.

Timetabling hours
Lectures times vary, according to course.
Modules cannot be studied that require attending only morning lectures.

Accommodation and childcare
Accommodation is available:

Specifically for mature students	No
For mature students with families	No

The institution does have crèche/childcare facilities.

General
The Mature Students' Society organises social activities and events for mature students.

Bridgwater College
Bath Road
Bridgwater
Somerset TA6 4PZ
Phone: 01278 441234
Fax: 01278 444363
Email: information@bridgwater.ac.uk
Website: www.bridgwater.ac.uk
Total number of students at institution: 13,000
Total number of mature students: 11,000

Student Support Officer
Simon Thomson
Phone: 01278 455464 ext. 360
Fax: 01278 444363
Email: thomsons@bridgwater.ac.uk

Applications
General entry qualifications that are considered acceptable for mature
applicants without the normal standard entry qualifications depend on the
level of the course.
The institution does not interview all mature applicants.

Funding
There are no specific mature student bursaries available over and above the
national funds.

Study
Negotiated flexible learning is available on some courses.
It is available to:

Full-time students	Yes
Part-time students	Yes
Distance Learning students	Yes

Timetabling hours
Lecture times vary.

Accommodation and childcare
Accommodation is available:

Specifically for mature students	No
For mature students with families	No

The institution does have crèche/childcare facilities.
Spaces are not always available.
There is a childminding network.

General

There are no societies or organised social activities for mature students.
There is online information specifically for mature students on the 'Adult'
pages.

University of Bristol

Senate House
Tyndall Avenue
Bristol
BS8 1TH
Phone: 0117 928 9000
Website: www.bristol.ac.uk
Total number of students at institution: 10,000 full-time
Total number of mature students: approximately 10 per cent of
undergraduate intake

Mature Students' Access Adviser

Betsy Bowerman
Phone: 0117 928 8862
Fax: 0117 928 9146
Email: e.bowerman@bristol.ac.uk

Applications

General entry qualifications that are considered acceptable for mature
applicants without the normal standard entry qualifications:

Access Course	Yes – depending on course.
Entrance exam	No

Other mature students' applications are considered individually. Evidence
of recent study usually required.

The institution does not interview all mature applicants.

Funding

There are no specific mature student bursaries available over and above the national funds.

Study

Negotiated flexible learning is not available on most courses.

Timetabling hours

Lectures are timetabled between 9am and 5pm.

Accommodation and childcare

Accommodation is available:

Specifically for mature students	No
For mature students with families	Yes – a small number of flats for couples and families with up to two small children

The institution does have crèche/childcare facilities.
There are 40 spaces.

General

There are societies or organised social activities for mature students.
There is online information specifically for mature students under 'M' in the A–Z index and under Support Services on the main website.

British College of Osteopathic Medicine

Lief House
120-122 Finchley Road
London
NW3 5HR
Phone: 020 7435 6464
Fax: 020 7431 3630
Email: registrar@bcom.ac.uk
Website: www.bcom.ac.uk

Total number of students at institution: 220
Total number of mature students: 150

Student Support Officer

Phone: 020 7435 6464
Email: registrar@bcom.ac.uk

Applications

General entry qualifications that are considered acceptable for mature applicants without the normal standard entry qualifications:

Access Course	Yes
Essay submission	No
Entrance exam	No
APEL/APL	Yes

The institution does not interview all mature applicants.

Funding

There are no specific mature student bursaries available over and above the national funds.

Study

Negotiated flexible learning is available on some courses, but only to full-time students.

Timetabling hours

Lectures are timetabled between 9am and 6pm.
Modules cannot be studied that require attending only morning lectures.

Accommodation and childcare

Accommodation is available:

Specifically for mature students	No
For mature students with families	No

The institution does not have crèche/childcare facilities.

General

There are no societies or organised social activities for mature students.
Those with queries about entry requirements or course details are welcome to contact Matthew Taylor, the academic registrar.

British School of Osteopathy

275 Borough High Street
London
SE1 1JE
Phone: 020 7407 0222
Fax: 020 7089 5300
Email: admissions@bso.ac.uk
Website: www.bso.ac.uk
Total number of students at institution: 429
Total number of mature students: 364 (over age 21)

Mature Students' Officer/Student Support Officer

Patricia Costall
Phone: 020 7089 5303
Fax: 020 7089 5300
Email: p.costall@bso.ac.uk

Applications

General entry qualifications that are considered acceptable for mature
applicants without the normal standard entry qualifications:

Access Course	Yes
Essay submission	No
Entrance exam	No
APEL/APL	Yes
Other	Each mature applicant is considered individually.

The institution does interview all mature applicants.

Funding

There are no specific mature student bursaries available over and above the
national funds.

Study

Negotiated flexible learning is not available on most courses.

Timetabling hours

Lectures are timetabled between 8.30am and 6.30pm.

Modules cannot be studied that require attending only morning lectures.

Accommodation and childcare

Accommodation is available:

Specifically for mature students	No
For mature students with families	No

The institution does not have crèche/childcare facilities.

General

There are no societies or organised social activities for mature students.
There is no online information specifically for mature students.
The majority of students at the British School of Osteopathy are over 21 years old; therefore, as an institution we are sensitive to the needs and concerns of mature applicants.

Brockenhurst College

Lyndhurst Road
Brockenhurst
Hampshire
SO42 7ZE
Phone: 01590 625555
Fax: 01590 625526
Website: www.brock.ac.uk
Total number of students at institution: 2,400
Total number of mature students: (part-time) 6,500

Mature Students' Officer

Nancey Copley
Phone: 01590 625513
Fax: 01590 625573
Email: ncopley@brock.ac.uk

Applications

General entry qualifications that are considered acceptable for mature applicants without the normal standard entry qualifications:

Access Course	No
Essay submission	No
Entrance exam	No
APEL/APL	No

Entry requirements depend on the course.

The institution does interview all mature applicants.

Funding

There are no specific mature student bursaries available over and above the national funds.

Study

Negotiated flexible learning is not available on most courses.

Timetabling hours

Lectures are timetabled between 9am and 4.20pm.

Modules cannot be studied that require attending only morning lectures.

Accommodation and childcare

Accommodation is available:

Specifically for mature students	No
For mature students with families	No

The institution does have crèche/childcare facilities: Highwood Nursery, which is owned and run by the college.

There are 74 spaces.

Spaces are always available.

General

There are no societies or organised social activities for mature students.
There is online information specifically for mature students on the Adult Student page of the website.

Brockenhurst College is essentially a sixth form college with some HND/Foundation Degree/Access provision with a large part-time student group.

Brunel University
Uxbridge
Middlesex
UB8 3PH
Phone: 01895 274000
Fax: 01895 232806
Website: www.brunel.ac.uk
Total number of students at institution: 13,402
Total number of mature students: 3,984

Applications
General entry qualifications that are considered acceptable for mature applicants without the normal standard entry qualifications:

Access Course	Yes
Essay submission	Yes
Entrance exam	Yes
APEL/APL	Yes

The institution does not interview all mature applicants.

Funding
There are no specific mature student bursaries available over and above the national funds.

Study
Negotiated flexible learning is not available on most courses.

Timetabling hours
Lectures are timetabled between 9.00am and 5.00pm.
Modules cannot be studied that require attending only morning lectures.

Accommodation and childcare
Accommodation is available:

Specifically for mature students	Yes
For mature students with families	No

The institution does not have crèche/childcare facilities.

General
There are societies or organised social activities for mature students. There is a Mature Students' Society.

Buckinghamshire Chilterns University College (BCUC)
Queen Alexandra Road
High Wycombe
Buckinghamshire
HP11 2JZ
Phone: 01494 524492
Fax: 01494 524392
Email: advice@bcuc.ac.uk
Website: www.bcuc.ac.uk
Total number of students at institution: 8,865
Total number of mature students: 4,972

Student Support Officer
Mohammed Adrees
Phone: 01494 603051
Fax: 01494 603189
Email: madrees01@bcuc.ac.uk

Applications
General entry qualifications that are considered acceptable for mature applicants without the normal standard entry qualifications:

Access Course	Yes
Essay submission	No
Entrance exam	No
APEL/APL	Yes

The institution does not interview all mature applicants.

Funding
There are no specific mature student bursaries available over and above the national funds.

Study
Negotiated flexible learning is available on some courses, but only to part-time students.

Timetabling hours

Lectures are timetabled between 9am and 9.30pm.

Modules cannot be studied that require attending only morning lectures.

Accommodation and childcare

Accommodation is available:

Specifically for mature students	No
For mature students with families	No

The institution does not have crèche/childcare facilities.

General

Visit www.bcsu.net for details of societies and organised social activities. There is no online information specifically for mature students.

Burton College

Lichfield Street
Burton on Trent
Staffordshire
DE14 3RL
Phone: 01283 494400
Fax: 01283 494800
Website: www.burton-college.ac.uk
Total number of students at institution: 10,000
Total number of mature students: 8,000

Student Support Officer

Anthony Hemmings/Claire Thomas
Phone: 01283 494475
Fax: 01283 494800

Applications

General entry qualifications that are considered acceptable for mature applicants without the normal standard entry qualifications:

Access Course	Yes
APEL/APL	Yes

Other	Interview and relevant experience.

Funding
There are no specific mature student bursaries available over and above the national funds.

Study
Negotiated flexible learning is available on most courses.
It is available to:

Part-time students	Yes
Distance Learning students	Yes

Timetabling hours
Lectures are timetabled between 9.30am and 9pm.
Modules can be studied that require attending only morning lectures.

Accommodation and childcare
Accommodation is available:

Specifically for mature students	No
For mature students with families	No

The institution does have crèche/childcare facilities.
Spaces are not always available.

Camberwell College of Arts
Peckham Road
London
SE5 8UF
Phone: 020 7514 6302
Fax: 020 7514 6310
Email: enquiries@camb.linst.ac.uk
Website: www.camb.linst.ac.uk

Student Support Officer
Phone: 020 7514 6354

Fax: 020 7514 6310
Email: d.johnson@camb.linst.ac.uk

Applications

General entry qualifications that are considered acceptable for mature applicants without the normal standard entry qualifications:

Access Course	Yes
Other	Relevant work experience.

Funding

There are no specific mature student bursaries available over and above the national funds.

Study

Negotiated flexible learning is available on courses in exceptional circumstances.

Timetabling hours

Lectures are timetabled between 10am and 6pm.
Modules can possibly be studied that require attending only morning lectures.

Accommodation and childcare

Accommodation is available:

Specifically for mature students	No
For mature students with families	No

The institution does have crèche/childcare facilities.
The crèche is off-site – please call 020 7514 6528 for further details.

General

There are no societies or organised social activities for mature students.
There is a small section of online information specifically for mature students in the Student Information section.

Canterbury Christ Church University College

North Holmes Road
Canterbury
Kent
CT1 1QU
Phone: 01227 767700
Fax: 01227 470442
Website: www.cant.ac.uk
Total number of mature students: 84 per cent of students are over 21 years old; 56 per cent of students are over 30 years old

Director of Student Support

Phone: 01227 782234
Fax: 01227 767279
Email: studentsupport@cant.ac.uk

Applications

General entry qualifications that are considered acceptable for mature applicants without the normal standard entry qualifications:

Access Course	Yes
Essay submission	No
Entrance exam	No
APEL/APL	Yes

The institution does interview all mature applicants.

Funding

There are no specific mature student bursaries available over and above the national funds, except for research students over the age of 26.

Study

Negotiated flexible learning is not available on most courses.

Timetabling hours

Lectures are timetabled between 9am and 7pm for the normal timetable, 6pm and 9pm for evening study, and in some cases there are weekend classes.
Modules can be studied that require attending only morning lectures, depending on option choice in years two and three.

Accommodation and childcare

Accommodation is available:

Specifically for mature students	Yes
For mature students with families	No

The institution does have crèche/childcare facilities and there are close links with other local childcare providers.
There are 20 spaces at Canterbury Day Nursery.
Spaces are not always available.

General

There are societies or organised social activities for mature students.
These are organised on an ad hoc basis by the mature students' officer of the students' union.
There is online information specifically for mature students, which is specifically for Thanet Campus – search for 'Mature Students' on the home page.

Capel Manor College

Bullsmoor Lane
Enfield
Middlesex
EN1 4RQ
Phone: 020 8366 4442
Fax: 01992 717544
Email: enquiries@capel.ac.uk
Website: www.capel.ac.uk
Total number of students at institution: 2,000
Total number of mature students: 1,400

Student Services Manager

Phone: 020 8366 4442
Fax: 01992 710312
Email: brenda.osakwe@capel.co.uk

Applications

General entry qualifications that are considered acceptable for mature applicants without the normal standard entry qualifications:

Access Course	Yes
Essay submission	No
Entrance exam	No
APEL/APL	Yes

The institution does interview all full-time and some part-time mature applicants.

Funding

There are no specific mature student bursaries available over and above the national funds.

Study

Negotiated flexible learning is not available on most courses.

Timetabling hours

Lectures are timetabled between 9am and 4pm or between 7.30am and 9.30pm or between 6.30am and 9.30pm.

Modules cannot be studied that require attending only morning lectures.

Accommodation and childcare

Accommodation is available:

Specifically for mature students	Yes – for students over 18 years of age.
For mature students with families	No

The institution does not have crèche/childcare facilities.

General

There are no societies or organised social activities for mature students.

There is no online information specifically for mature students, but the website contains information for all students.

Cardiff University

PO Box 927
50 Park Place
Cardiff
CF10 3UA

Phone: 029 2087 4404
Fax: 029 2087 6982
Email: admissions@cardiff.ac.uk
Website: www.cardiff.ac.uk
Total number of students at institution: 15,600
Total number of mature students: 1,872

Mature Students' Officer
Phone: 029 2078 1400

Applications
Entry qualifications vary depending on the course applied for.
The institution does not interview all mature applicants.

Accommodation and childcare
Accommodation is available:

Specifically for mature students	No
For mature students with families	Yes – there is limited accommodation for couples and families.

The institution does have crèche/childcare facilities.
Spaces are not always available.

General
There is online information specifically for mature students at
www.cf.ac.uk/courses/undergraduate/mature
A Guide for Mature Students is available.

University of Central England in Birmingham
Perry Barr
Birmingham
B42 2SU
Phone: 0121 331 5000
Fax: 0121 331 6740
Email: info@ucechoices.com

Website: www.uce.ac.uk

Total number of students at institution: 23,740

Applications

General entry qualifications that are considered acceptable for mature applicants without the normal standard entry qualifications:

Access Course	Yes
Essay submission	No
Entrance exam	No
APEL/APL	No

The institution does not interview all mature applicants.

Funding

There are no specific mature student bursaries available over and above the national funds.

Study

Negotiated flexible learning is available on most courses.
It is available to:

Full-time students	Yes
Part-time students	Yes

Timetabling hours

Lectures are timetabled between 9am and 9pm.
Depending on the course, some modules might be able to be studied that require attending only morning lectures.

Accommodation and childcare

Accommodation is available:

Specifically for mature students	No
For mature students with families	Yes – family/couple room.

The institution does have crèche/childcare facilities.
The number of spaces varies.
Spaces are not always available.

General
There are no societies or organised social activities for mature students.
There is no online information specifically for mature students.

University of Central Lancashire
Fylde Road
Preston
PR1 2HE
Phone: 01772 201201
Fax: 01772 894954
Email: cenquiries@uclan.ac.uk
Website: www.uclan.ac.uk
Total number of students at institution: 29,436
Total number of mature students: 18,222

Mature Students' Officer
Phone: 01772 892416
Fax: 01772 894954
Email: brimmer@uclan.ac.uk

Applications
General entry qualifications that are considered acceptable for mature
applicants without the normal standard entry qualifications:

Access Course	Yes
Essay submission	Yes
Entrance exam	Yes
APEL/APL	Yes

The institution does not interview all mature applicants.

Funding
There are no specific mature student bursaries available over and above the
national funds.

Study
Negotiated flexible learning is available on most courses.
It is available to:

Full-time students	Yes
Part-time students	Yes
Distance Learning students	Yes

Timetabling hours
Lectures are timetabled between 9am and 9pm.
Modules can be studied that require attending only morning lectures.

Accommodation and childcare
Accommodation is available:

Specifically for mature students	No
For mature students with families	No

The institution does have crèche/childcare facilities.
Spaces are always available.

General
There are no societies or organised social activities for mature students.
There is online information specifically for mature students at
www.uclan.ac.uk/courses/guide/mature.htm

Central Saint Martins College of Art and Design
Southampton Row
London
WC1B 4AP
Phone: 020 7514 7000
Fax: 020 7514 7254
Email: info@csm.linst.ac.uk
Website: www.csm.linst.ac.uk

Head of Student Advice and Guidance
Paul Rossi
Phone: 020 7514 6230
Fax: 020 7514 6219
Email: student.services@linst.ac.uk

Applications
General entry qualifications that are considered acceptable for mature
applicants without the normal standard entry qualifications:

Access Course	Yes
Essay submission	No
Entrance exam	No
APEL/APL	No

The institution does not interview all mature applicants.

Funding
There are no specific mature student bursaries available over and above the national funds.

Study
Negotiated flexible learning is not available on most courses.

Timetabling hours
Lectures are timetabled between 9am and 7pm.
Modules cannot be studied that require attending only morning lectures.

Accommodation and childcare
Accommodation is available:

Specifically for mature students	No
For mature students with families	No

The institution does have crèche/childcare facilities.
There are 34 spaces.
Spaces are not always available.
The day nursery is open from 8.30am to 6pm Monday to Friday during term time.

General
There are no societies or organised social activities for mature students.
There is no online information specifically for mature students.

Central School of Speech and Drama
Embassy Theatre
Eton Avenue
London
NW3 3HY

Phone: 020 7722 8183
Fax: 020 7722 4132
Website: www.cssd.ac.uk
Total number of students at institution: 650
Total number of mature students: approximately 300

Student Support Officer

Keith Silvester
Phone: 020 7559 3933
Fax: 020 7559 3998
Email: k.silvester@cssd.ac.uk

Applications

General entry qualifications that are considered acceptable for mature applicants without the normal standard entry qualifications:

APEL/APL	Yes
Other	Audition, interview.

The institution does not interview all mature applicants.

Funding

There are specific mature student bursaries available over and above the national funds.

Study

Negotiated flexible learning is available on some courses.
It is available to:

Full-time students	No
Part-time students	Yes
Other	Varies according to course.

Timetabling hours

Lectures are timetabled between 9am and 6pm, depending on the course. Modules can be studied that require attending only morning lectures.

Accommodation and childcare

Accommodation is available:

Specifically for mature students	No
For mature students with families	Yes

The institution does not have crèche/childcare facilities.
Financial support for childcare is offered where eligible.

General
There are no societies or organised social activities for mature students.
There is no specific online information for mature students, but the
institution's Student's Companion guide (on the website) contains useful
material.

University College Chester
Parkgate Road
Chester
Cheshire
CH1 4BJ
Phone: 01244 375444
Fax: 01244 392820
Email: enquiries@chester.ac.uk
Website: www.chester.ac.uk
Total number of students at institution: 10,500
Total number of mature students: c. 5,000

Student Support Officer
Mr Jan Turnbull
Phone: 01244 375444
Fax: 01244 392821
Email: j.turnbull@chester.ac.uk

Applications
General entry qualifications that are considered acceptable for mature
applicants without the normal standard entry qualifications:

Access Course	Yes
Essay submission	No
Entrance exam	No
APEL/APL	Yes

The institution does not interview all mature applicants.

Funding
There are no specific mature student bursaries available over and above the national funds.

Study
Negotiated flexible learning is available on most courses to part-time students.

Timetabling hours
Lectures are timetabled between 9am and 6pm.
Modules cannot be studied that require attending only morning lectures.

Accommodation and childcare
Accommodation is available:

Specifically for mature students	Yes – there are two self-contained flats that are ideal for mature students.
For mature students with families	No

The institution does have crèche/childcare facilities.
Spaces are not always available.

General
There are lots of clubs and social activities open to all students.

Chesterfield College
Infirmary Road
Chesterfield
Derbyshire
S41 7MG
Phone: 01246 500500
Fax: 01246 500587
Total number of students at institution: 33,000

Student Support Officer
Joe Marsden
Phone: 01246 500534

Fax: 01246 500587
Email: marsdenj@chesterfield.ac.uk

Applications

General entry qualifications that are considered acceptable for mature applicants without the normal standard entry qualifications:

Access Course	Yes

The institution does interview all mature applicants.

Funding

There are no specific mature student bursaries available over and above the national funds.

Study

Negotiated flexible learning is not available on most courses.
Distance learning is available.

Timetabling hours

Lectures are timetabled between 9am and 9pm.
Modules cannot be studied that require attending only morning lectures.

Accommodation and childcare

Accommodation is available:

Specifically for mature students	No
For mature students with families	No

The institution does have crèche/childcare facilities.
Spaces are not always available.

General

There are no societies or organised social activities for mature students.

University College Chichester

College Lane
Chichester
PO19 6PE
Phone: 01243 816000

Fax: 01243 816078
Email: admissions@ucc.ac.uk
Website: www.ucc.ac.uk

Assistant Principal

Dr Sarah Gilroy
Phone: 01243 816030
Fax: 01243 816080
Email: s.gilroy@ucc.ac.uk

Applications

General entry qualifications that are considered acceptable for mature
applicants without the normal standard entry qualifications:

Access Course	Yes
Essay submission	Yes
Entrance exam	No
APEL/APL	Yes

The institution does not interview all mature applicants.

Funding

There are no specific mature student bursaries available over and above the
national funds.

Study

Negotiated flexible learning is available on most courses.

Timetabling hours

Modules can be studied that require attending only morning lectures.

Accommodation and childcare

Accommodation is available:

Specifically for mature students	No
For mature students with families	No

The institution does not have crèche/childcare facilities.

General

There are no societies or organised social activities for mature students.
There is no online information specifically for mature students.
Approximately 30 per cent of University College Chichester students are

mature students. The institution says it offers a supportive environment for mature students.

City of Bristol College

College Green Centre
St George's Road
Bristol
BS1 5UA
Phone: 0117 904 5000
Fax: 0117 904 5051
Email: enquiries@cityofbristol.ac.uk
Website: www.cityofbristol.ac.uk
Total number of students at institution: 30,000
Total number of mature students: 25,000

Student Support Officer

Andrew Burton
Phone: 0117 904 5000
Fax: 0117 904 5051
Email: enquiries@cityofbristol.ac.uk

Applications

General entry qualifications that are considered acceptable for mature applicants without the normal standard entry qualifications:

Other	Varies according to course.

The institution does not interview all mature applicants.

Funding

There are no specific mature student bursaries available over and above the national funds.

Study

Negotiated flexible learning is available on some courses.
It is available to:

Full-time students	No
Part-time students	Yes
Distance Learning students	Yes

Timetabling hours

Lectures are timetabled between 9am and 7pm.
Modules cannot be studied that require attending only morning lectures.

Accommodation and childcare

Accommodation is available:

Specifically for mature students	Yes
For mature students with families	No

The institution does have crèche/childcare facilities.
Please ring for details about spaces etc.

General

There are societies or organised social activities for mature students.
These are run by the Students' Union.
There is no online information specifically for mature students at present,
but there is a forthcoming adult learning section on the new website.

City College Manchester

141 Barlow Moor Road
West Didsbury
Manchester
M20 2PQ
Phone: 0161 957 1790
Fax: 0161 446 1185
Email: admissions@ccm.ac.uk
Website: www.ccm.ac.uk
Approximately one third of all the students of HE at this institution are
aged 21+

Guidance Adviser

Phone: 0161 957 1735
Email: cmacdonald@ccm.ac.uk

Applications

General entry qualifications that are considered acceptable for mature applicants without the normal standard entry qualifications:

Access Course	Yes
Essay submission	Yes
Entrance exam	No
APEL/APL	Yes
Other	Transfer from HNC to HND/degree.

The institution does not interview all mature applicants.

Funding

There are specific mature student bursaries available over and above the national funds. The college makes some of its access funds available to mature students.

Study

Negotiated flexible learning is not available on most courses.

Timetabling hours

Lectures are timetabled between 9am and 5pm.

Accommodation and childcare

Accommodation is available:

Specifically for mature students	No – the college has no accommodation, but the accommodation office helps students to find housing.
For mature students with families	No – the college has no accommodation, but the

	accommodation office helps students to find housing.

The institution does have crèche/childcare facilities.
There are 160 spaces.
Spaces are not always available.

General
There are no societies or organised social activities for mature students.
There is no online information specifically for mature students.

City and Islington College
The Marlborough Building
383 Holloway Road
London
N7 0RN
Phone: 020 7700 9200
Fax: 020 7700 9222
Email: courseinfo@candi.ac.uk
Website: www.candi.ac.uk
Total number of HE students at institution: 100
Total number of HE mature students: 65

Student Support Officer
Phone: 020 7700 9333

Applications
General entry qualifications that are considered acceptable for mature applicants without the normal standard entry qualifications:

Access Course	Yes
Entrance exam	Yes
APEL/APL	Yes

The institution does interview all mature applicants.

Funding
There are no specific mature student bursaries available over and above the national funds.

Study
Negotiated flexible learning is not available on most courses.

Timetabling hours
Lectures are timetabled between 9am and 8pm.
Modules cannot be studied that require attending only morning lectures.

Accommodation and childcare
Accommodation is available:

Specifically for mature students	No
For mature students with families	No

The institution does have crèche/childcare facilities.
Spaces are not always available.

General
There are no societies or organised social activities for mature students.

Cleveland College of Art and Design
Green Lane
Linthorpe
Middlesbrough
TS5 7RJ
Phone: 01642 288000
Fax: 01642 288828
Website: www.ccad.ac.uk

Student Support Officer
Joey McGurk
Phone: 01642 288000
Email: joey.mcgurk@ccad.ac.uk

Applications
General entry qualifications that are considered acceptable for mature applicants without the normal standard entry qualifications:

Other	Students need a portfolio of work.

The institution does interview all mature applicants.

Funding
There are no specific mature student bursaries available over and above the national funds.

Timetabling hours
Lectures are timetabled between 9.30am and 6.30pm.
Modules cannot be studied that require attending only morning lectures.

Accommodation and childcare
Accommodation is available:

Specifically for mature students	No
For mature students with families	No

The institution does not have crèche/childcare facilities.

General
There are no societies or organised social activities for mature students.
There is no online information specifically for mature students.

Colchester Institute
Sheepen Road
Colchester
Essex
CO3 3LL
Phone: 01206 518000
Fax: 01206 763041
Website: www.colchester.ac.uk
Total number of students at institution: 12,000

Students' Union
Phone: 01206 518705
Fax: 01206 573838
Email: student.union@colchester.ac.uk

Applications

General entry qualifications that are considered acceptable for mature applicants without the normal standard entry qualifications:

Access Course	Yes

Funding

There are no specific mature student bursaries available over and above the national funds.

Study

Negotiated flexible learning is not available on most courses.
It is available to:

Full-time students	No
Part-time students	No
Distance Learning students	Yes

Timetabling hours

Lecture times vary.

Accommodation and childcare

Accommodation is available:

Specifically for mature students	No
For mature students with families	No

The institution does have crèche/childcare facilities.
There are 24 spaces.
Spaces are not always available.

General

There will be societies or organised social activities for mature students as of September 2003.

University College Cork

College Road
Cork
Republic of Ireland

Phone: 00 353 21 490 3000
Fax: 00 353 21 490 3233
Email: admissions@ucc.ie
Website: www.ucc.ie
Total number of students at institution: 14,500
Total number of mature students: 900 full-time and 2,000 part-time

Mature Students' Officer

Phone: 00 353 21 490 3670
Fax: 00 353 21 490 3233
Email: c.quinlan@ucc.ie

Applications

General entry qualifications that are considered acceptable for mature applicants without the normal standard entry qualifications:

Essay submission	Yes
Entrance exam	Yes
Other	Interview

The institution does not interview all mature applicants.

Funding

There are specific mature student bursaries available over and above the national funds.

Study

Negotiated flexible learning is available on some courses.
It is available to:

Full-time students	No
Part-time students	Yes
Distance Learning students	Yes

Timetabling hours

Lectures are timetabled between 8am and 7pm for full-time students and between 5.30pm and 10.30pm for part-time students.
Modules cannot be studied that require attending only morning lectures.

Accommodation and childcare

Accommodation is available:

Specifically for mature students	No
For mature students with families	No

The institution does have crèche/childcare facilities.

There are 33 spaces.

Spaces are not always available.

A new crèche, which will provide 80 spaces, is under construction and is due for completion in January 2005.

General

There are societies or organised social activities for mature students – the Mature Student Society.

There is online information specifically for mature students.

There are support services available for mature students during the year.

Cranfield University

Shrivenham
Swindon
SL6 8LA
Phone: 01793 785693
Email: stservices@rmcs.cranfield.ac.uk
Website: www.cranfield.ac.uk

Student Support Officer

Student Services Unit
Email: stservices@rmcs.cranfield.ac.uk

Applications

General entry qualifications that are considered acceptable for mature applicants without the normal standard entry qualifications:

Access Course	Yes

The institution does not interview all mature applicants.

Funding

There are no specific mature student bursaries available over and above the national funds.

Study

Negotiated flexible learning is not available on most courses.

Timetabling hours

Lectures are timetabled between 9am and 5pm.

Modules cannot be studied that require attending only morning lectures.

Accommodation and childcare

Accommodation is available:

Specifically for mature students	No
For mature students with families	No

The institution does have crèche/childcare facilities.

Spaces are not always available.

Spaces must be booked approximately six months in advance.

General

There are no societies or organised social activities for mature students.

Crawley College

College Road
Crawley
West Sussex
RH10 1NR
Phone: 01293 442200
Fax: 01293 442399
Email: information@crawley-college.ac.uk
Website: www.crawley-college.ac.uk
Total number of students at institution: 14,770
Total number of mature students: 12,555

Student Support Officer

Laura Woodgate
Phone: 01293 442204
Fax: 01293 442399
Email: lwoodgate@crawley-college.ac.uk

Applications

General entry qualifications that are considered acceptable for mature applicants without the normal standard entry qualifications:

Access Course	Yes
Entrance exam	Yes
Other	Industry experience, successful interview.

The institution does interview all mature applicants.

Funding

There are no specific mature student bursaries available over and above the national funds.

Study

Negotiated flexible learning is available on some courses.
It is available to:

Full-time students	No
Part-time students	Yes
Distance Learning students	Yes

Timetabling hours

Modules can be studied that require attending only morning lectures.

Accommodation and childcare

Accommodation is available:

Specifically for mature students	No – we do have accommodation, but it is with host families on a paying basis.
For mature students with families	No

The institution does not have crèche/childcare facilities.

General

There are societies or organised social activities for mature students. Student Services are happy to provide information and answer any questions prospective mature students may have.

Croydon College

Fairfield Campus
College Road
Croydon
CR9 1DX
Phone: 020 8686 5700
Fax: 020 8760 5880
Email: info@croydon.ac.uk
Website: www.croydon.ac.uk
Total number of students at institution: 14,000
Total number of mature students: 10,000

Student Support Officer

Phone: 020 8760 5995
Fax: 020 8760 5880
Email: jenkil@croydon.ac.uk

Applications

General entry qualifications that are considered acceptable for mature applicants without the normal standard entry qualifications:

Access Course	Yes
Essay submission	Yes
Entrance exam	No
APEL/APL	Yes

The institution does not interview all mature applicants.

Funding

There are no specific mature student bursaries available over and above the national funds.

Study

Negotiated flexible learning is available on most courses.

It is available to:

Full-time students	Yes
Part-time students	Yes
Distance Learning students	Yes

Timetabling hours
Modules can be studied that require attending only morning lectures.

Accommodation and childcare
Accommodation is available:

Specifically for mature students	No
For mature students with families	No

The institution does not have crèche/childcare facilities.

General
There are no societies or organised social activities for mature students.

Cumbria Institute of the Arts
Brampton Road
Carlisle
Cumbria
CA3 9AY
Phone: 01228 400300
Fax: 01228 514491
Email: info@cumbria.ac.uk
Website: www.cumbria.ac.uk
Total number of students at institution: 1,700
Total number of mature students: 250

Admissions Officer
Phone: 01228 400300
Fax: 01228 514491
Email: admissions@cumbria.ac.uk

Applications
General entry qualifications that are considered acceptable for mature applicants without the normal standard entry qualifications:

Access Course	Yes

The institution does interview all mature applicants.

Funding
There are no specific mature student bursaries available over and above the national funds.

Study
Negotiated flexible learning is available on most courses.
It is available to:

Part-time students	Yes
Distance Learning students	No

Accommodation and childcare
Accommodation is available:

Specifically for mature students	No
For mature students with families	No

The institution does not have crèche/childcare facilities.

General
There are no societies or organised social activities for mature students.

Dearne Valley College
Manvers Park
Wath-upon-Dearne
Rotherham
S63 7EW
Phone: 01709 513333
Fax: 01709 513110
Email: learn@dearne-coll.ac.uk
Website: www.dearne-coll.ac.uk

Student Support Officer
Su Connell
Phone: 01709 513333

Fax: 01709 513110
Email: sconnell@dearne-coll.ac.uk

Applications
The institution does not interview all mature applicants.

Study
Negotiated flexible learning is not available on most courses.

Accommodation and childcare
Accommodation is available:

Specifically for mature students	No
For mature students with families	No

The institution does have crèche/childcare facilities.
Spaces are not always available.

General
The students' union organises social activities for mature students.

Denbigh Community College
Crown Lane
Denbigh
Denbighshire
North Wales
LL16 3SY
Phone: 01745 812812
Fax: 01745 816356
Email: denbigh.admissions@llandrillo.ac.uk
Website: www.llandrillo.ac.uk/denbigh
Total number of students at institution: c. 835
Total number of mature students: c. 835

Study/Basic Skills Facilitator
Melina Jones
Phone: 01745 812812 ext. 655
Fax: 01745 816356
Email: denbigh.admissions@llandrillo.ac.uk

Applications

General entry qualifications that are considered acceptable for mature applicants without the normal standard entry qualifications:

Access Course	No
Essay submission	No
Entrance exam	No
APEL/APL	No
Other	All students are considered on individual experience and merit.

The institution does not interview all mature applicants.

Funding

There are no specific mature student bursaries available over and above the national funds.

Study

Negotiated flexible learning is available on most courses.
It is available to:

Full-time students	Yes
Part-time students	Yes
Distance Learning students	Yes

Timetabling hours

Lectures are timetabled between 9am and 9pm.

General

There are no societies or organised social activities for mature students.
There is no online information specifically for mature students.
Denbigh Community College prides itself on its supportive environment, with student support services and advice and guidance for all students.

Dudley College
The Broadway
Dudley
West Midlands
DY1 4AS
Phone: 01384 363000
Fax: 01384 363311
Website: www.dudleycol.ac.uk
Total number of students at institution: 11,000

Guidance Officers, Student Services
Phone: 01384 363363
Fax: 01384 363311
Email: student.services@dudleycol.ac.uk

Applications
General entry qualifications that are considered acceptable for mature applicants without the normal standard entry qualifications:

Access Course	Yes
APEL/APL	Yes

The institution does interview all full-time mature applicants.

Funding
There are no specific mature student bursaries available over and above the national funds.

Study
Access programmes for full-time, part-time and distance learning over-19-year-olds can cater for individual timetables and negotiated flexible learning.

Timetabling hours
Lectures are timetabled between 9am and 9.30pm.
Modules cannot be studied that require attending only morning lectures.

Accommodation and childcare
Accommodation is available:

Specifically for mature students	No
For mature students with families	No

The institution does have crèche/childcare facilities.
There are six spaces for the under twos and 20 spaces for ages two and above.
Spaces are not always available.

General
There are no societies or organised social activities for mature students.

Dundee College
Old Glamis Road
Dundee
DD3 8LE
Phone: 01382 834826
Email: k.neades@dundeecoll.ac.uk
Website: www.dundeecoll.ac.uk
Total number of students at institution: 2,700
Total number of mature students: 1,500

Student Support Officer
Phone: 01382 834826
Email: k.neades@dundeecoll.ac.uk

Applications
General entry qualifications that are considered acceptable for mature applicants without the normal standard entry qualifications:

Access Course	Yes
Essay submission	Yes
APEL/APL	Yes

The institution does not interview all mature applicants.

Funding
There are specific mature student bursaries available over and above the national funds.

Study
Negotiated flexible learning is available on most courses.
It is available to:

Full-time students	Yes
Part-time students	Yes
Distance Learning students	Yes

Timetabling hours

Lectures are timetabled between 9am and 9pm.

Modules can be studied that require attending only morning lectures.

Accommodation and childcare

Accommodation is available:

Specifically for mature students	Yes
For mature students with families	No

The institution does not have crèche/childcare facilities but does offer financial support for childcare.

General

There are societies or organised social activities for mature students via Student Association.

There is online information specifically for mature students.

University of Durham

University Office
Old Elvet
Durham
DH1 3HP
Phone: 0191 334 2000
Fax: 0191 334 6250
Website: www.dur.ac.uk
Total number of students at institution: 13,623
Total number of mature students: 583 undergraduate, 885 postgraduate

Student Financial Support Officer

Elizabeth Glossop
Phone: 0191 334 6116
Fax: 0191 334 6250
Email: e.l.glossop@durham.ac.uk

Applications

General entry qualifications that are considered acceptable for mature applicants without the normal standard entry qualifications:

Access Course	Yes
Essay submission	No
Entrance exam	No

The institution does not interview all mature applicants.

Funding

There are no specific mature student bursaries available over and above the national funds.

Study

Negotiated flexible learning is not available on most courses.

Timetabling hours

Lectures are timetabled between 9am and 6.15pm.
Modules cannot be studied that require attending only morning lectures.

Accommodation and childcare

Accommodation is available:

Specifically for mature students	No
For mature students with families	No

The institution does have crèche/childcare facilities.

General

There are societies or organised social activities for mature students.
St Cuthbert's Society is the college (Durham is a collegiate university) that many mature students attend.

University of East Anglia

Norwich
Norfolk
NR4 7TJ
Phone: 01603 456161
Fax: 01603 458596

Email: admissions@uea.ac.uk

Website: www.uea.ac.uk

Dean of Students' Office

Phone: 01603 593892

Fax: 01603 593454

Applications

General entry qualifications that are considered acceptable for mature applicants without the normal standard entry qualifications:

Access Course	Yes
APEL/APL	Yes
Other	Some schools of study require a written essay/ exam; contact the relevant school for details.

The institution does interview all mature applicants.

Study

Negotiated flexible learning is not available on most courses, but students can choose seminars timetabled to their needs.

Timetabling hours

Lectures are timetabled between 9am and 5pm for undergraduates. Modules can be studied that require attending only morning lectures.

Accommodation and childcare

Accommodation is available:

Specifically for mature students	Yes
For mature students with families	Yes – approximately 40 family accommodation units on campus.

The institution does have crèche/childcare facilities.

There are 106 spaces.

Spaces are not always available.

A weekly parent and children group is held at the university.

General

A mature students' society is currently being formed.

There is online information specifically for mature students at
www.uea.ac.uk/admissions/mature_students

Mature students should contact the relevant school of study and the Dean
of Students to discuss their individual needs.

University of East London

Barking Campus
Longbridge Road
Dagenham
Essex
RM8 2AS
Phone: 020 8223 2420
Fax: 020 8597 6987
Website: www.uel.ac.uk
Total number of students at institution: 14,000
Total number of mature students: 6,000

Mature Students' Officer

Nana Ackom-Mensah
Phone: 020 8223 2420
Fax: 020 8597 6987

Student Support Officer

Jacqueline Bourne
Phone: 020 8223 2420
Fax: 020 8597 6987

Applications

General entry qualifications that are considered acceptable for mature
applicants without the normal standard entry qualifications:

Access Course	Yes
Essay submission	Yes
Entrance exam	Yes
APEL/APL	Yes

The institution does not interview all mature applicants.

Funding

There are no specific mature student bursaries available over and above the national funds.

Study

Negotiated flexible learning is available on some courses.
It is available to:

Full-time students	No
Part-time students	Yes
Distance Learning students	Yes

Timetabling hours

Lectures are timetabled between 9am and 9pm.
Modules can be studied that require attending only morning lectures.

Accommodation and childcare

Accommodation is available:

Specifically for mature students	No
For mature students with families	No

The institution does have crèche/childcare facilities.
There are 50 spaces for two and a half to five-year-olds.
Spaces are not always available.

General

There are societies or organised social activities for mature students, which are run by the Mature Student Unit.
There is online information specifically for mature students.

East Surrey College
Gatton Point
Claremont Road
Redhill
Surrey
RH1 2JX
Phone: 01737 772611
Fax: 01737 768641
Email: studentservices@esc.ac.uk
Website: www.esc.ac.uk
Total number of students at institution: 3,000+
Total number of mature students: 1,000+

Student Services
Phone: 01737 788444
Fax: 01737 768641
Email: studentservices@esc.ac.uk

Applications
The institution does interview all mature applicants.

Funding
There are no specific mature student bursaries available over and above the national funds.

Study
Negotiated flexible learning is only available to distance learning students.

Timetabling hours
Lectures are timetabled between 9am and 6pm.
Modules can be studied that require attending only morning lectures.

Accommodation and childcare
Accommodation is available:

Specifically for mature students	No
For mature students with families	No

The institution does have crèche/childcare facilities.
There are 12 spaces.
Spaces are not always available and need to be booked.

General

There are no societies or organised social activities for mature students.
There is no online information specifically for mature students.

Easton College

Easton
Norwich
Norfolk
NR9 5DX
Phone: 01603 731200
Website: www.easton.ac.uk
Total number of students at institution: 500 full-time
Total number of mature students: 100 full-time

Information Centre

Phone: 01603 741438
Email: info@easton.ac.uk
All mature applications are considered and evaluated on an individual basis.
The institution does interview all mature applicants.

Funding

All students are eligible to apply to the College Access Fund.

Timetabling hours

Lectures are timetabled between 9.15am and 9.00pm.
Modules may possibly be studied that require attending only morning
lectures.

Accommodation and childcare

Accommodation is available:

Specifically for mature students	No
For mature students with families	No

The institution does not have crèche/childcare facilities.

Edge Hill College
St Helen's Road
Ormskirk
West Lancashire
L39 4QP
Phone: 01695 584255
Fax: 01695 577904
Email: berryp@edgehill.ac.uk
Website: www.edgehillsu.com

Academic and Welfare Officer
Stephanie Drysdale
Phone: 01695 584096
Email: drysdals@edgehill.ac.uk

Applications
General entry qualifications that are considered acceptable for mature applicants without the normal standard entry qualifications:

Access Course	Yes

The institution does interview all mature applicants.

Study
Negotiated flexible learning is available on some courses.

Timetabling hours
Lectures are timetabled between 9am and 5pm.
Modules can be studied that require attending only morning lectures.

Accommodation and childcare
Accommodation is available:

Specifically for mature students	No
For mature students with families	No

The institution does not have crèche/childcare facilities.

University of Essex

Wivenhoe Park
Colchester
Essex
CO4 3SQ
Phone: 01206 873333
Fax: 01206 873598
Email: admit@essex.ac.uk
Website: www.essex.ac.uk
Total number of students at institution: 6686
Total number of mature students: 18 per cent of undergraduates

Mature Students' Officer

Phone: 01206 863211
Fax: 01206 870915
Email: matureofficer@essex.ac.uk

Student Support Officer

Phone: 01206 872366
Fax: 01206 872367
Email: sso@essex.ac.uk

Applications

General entry qualifications that are considered acceptable for mature
applicants without the normal standard entry qualifications:

Access Course	Yes

Other Foundation degree/A-level applicants assessed on individual merit
and qualifications.

Funding

There are specific mature student bursaries available over and above the
national funds. Additional funding and bursaries (e.g. hardship funds) are
available to all students.

Study

Negotiated flexible learning is available, depending on the course.

Timetabling hours

Lectures are timetabled between 9am and 6pm.
Modules cannot be studied that require attending only morning lectures.

Accommodation and childcare

Accommodation is available:

Specifically for mature students	No

For mature students with families Yes – there is limited family accommodation.
The institution does have crèche/childcare facilities.
Spaces are always available.

General

There are societies or organised social activities for mature students.
The Mature Students' Society organises specific social events.
There is detailed online information specifically for mature students.

European School of Osteopathy

Boxley House
The Street
Boxley
Nr Maidstone
Kent
ME14 3DZ
Phone: 01622 671558
Fax: 01622 662165
Email: kellyrose@eso.ac.uk
Website: www.eso.ac.uk

Mature Students' Officer

Kelly Rose
Email: kellyrose@eso.ac.uk

Student Support Officer

Ms Shauna Black/Ms Sue Morton
Phone: 01622 671558
Fax: 01622 662165

Applications

General entry qualifications that are considered acceptable for mature applicants without the normal standard entry qualifications:

Access Course	Yes
Essay submission	No
Entrance exam	No
APEL/APL	No
Other	Science Access Course

The institution does interview all mature applicants.

Funding

There are no specific mature student bursaries available over and above the national funds.

Study

Negotiated flexible learning is not available on most courses.

Timetabling hours

Lectures are timetabled between 9.15am and 5.20pm.
Modules cannot be studied that require attending only morning lectures.

Accommodation and childcare

Accommodation is available:

Specifically for mature students	No
For mature students with families	No

The institution does not have crèche/childcare facilities.

General

There are no societies or organised social activities specifically for mature students.
There is no online information specifically for mature students.

University of Exeter

Northcote House
The Queen's Drive
Exeter
EX4 4QJ
Phone: 01392 263500
Fax: 01392 263108
Website: www.exeter.ac.uk

Total number of students at institution: 12,442
Total number of mature students: 3,500

Student Support Officer
Phone: 01392 263520
Email: welfare@guild.ex.ac.uk

Applications
General entry qualifications that are considered acceptable for mature applicants without the normal standard entry qualifications:

Access Course	Yes
Essay submission	Yes – on certain occasions.
Entrance exam	No
APEL/APL	Yes
Other	Depending on the individual: OU, HND, BTEC etc.

The institution does interview mature applicants if an offer is not made on the basis of an application.

Funding
There are specific mature student bursaries available over and above the national funds.

Study
Negotiated flexible learning is available on most courses.
It is available to:

Part-time students	Yes – DLL
Distance Learning students	Yes

Timetabling hours
Modules can be studied that require attending only morning lectures.

Accommodation and childcare
Accommodation is available:

Specifically for mature students	No

For mature students with families Yes – family flats.
The institution does have crèche/childcare facilities.
There are 42 spaces.
Spaces are not always available.

General
There are societies or organised social activities for mature students.
These are run by the Guild of Students.
There is online information specifically for mature students at
www.exeter.ac.uk/mature/

Fareham College
Bishopsfield Road
Fareham
Hants
PO14 1NH
Phone: 01329 815200
Fax: 01329 822483
Website: www.fareham.ac.uk

Mature Students' Officer
Chris Kirby
Phone: 01329 815200
Fax: 01329 822483
Email: chris.kirby@fareham.ac.uk

Student Support Officer
Angela Livermore
Phone: 01329 815200
Fax: 01329 822483
Email: angela.livermore@fareham.ac.uk

Applications
General entry qualifications that are considered acceptable for mature
applicants without the normal standard entry qualifications:

Access Course	Yes
Essay submission	Yes
Entrance exam	Yes
APEL/APL	Yes

The institution does interview all mature applicants.

Funding

There are no specific mature student bursaries available over and above the national funds.

Study

Negotiated flexible learning is not available on most courses.
It is available to:

Full-time students	No
Part-time students	Yes

Distance Learning students No

Timetabling hours

Lectures are timetabled between 9.00am and 9.30pm.
Modules can be studied that require attending only morning lectures.

Accommodation and childcare

Accommodation is available:

Specifically for mature students	No
For mature students with families	No

The institution does have crèche/childcare facilities.
There are two independently run nurseries on site.

General

There are no societies or organised social activities for mature students.
There is online information specifically for mature students, which can be found at www.fareham.ac.uk
Mature students are very welcome. Careers interviews are available.

Farnborough College of Technology

Boundary Road
Farnborough
Hampshire
GU14 6SB
Phone: 01252 407040

Fax: 01252 407041
Email: info@farn-ct.ac.uk
Website: www.farn-ct.ac.uk
Total number of students at institution: 12,614
Total number of mature students: (aged 19+) 11,057

Student Support Officer

Jose Harrap
Phone: 01252 407346
Fax: 01252 407041
Email: j.harrap@farn-ct.ac.uk

Applications

General entry qualifications that are considered acceptable for mature
applicants without the normal standard entry qualifications:

Access Course	Yes
APEL/APL	Yes

The institution does interview all mature applicants.

Funding

There are no specific mature student bursaries available over and above the
national funds.

Study

Negotiated flexible learning is available on most courses.
It is available to:

Part-time students	Yes
Distance Learning students	No

Timetabling hours

Lectures are timetabled between 9am and 9.30pm.

Accommodation and childcare

Accommodation is available:

Specifically for mature students	No
For mature students with families	No

The institution does have crèche/childcare facilities.

There are 33 spaces.

Spaces are not always available.

General

There are no societies or organised social activities for mature students.

There is no online information specifically for mature students.

The prospectus gives clear entry requirements for mature students applying for degree courses.

University of Glamorgan

Llantwit Road

Treforest

Pontypridd

Mid Glamorgan

CF37 1GY

Phone: 0800 716925 (from UK); +44 1443 828812 (from overseas)

Fax: 01443 480558

Email: enquiries@glam.ac.uk

Website: www.glam.ac.uk

Total number of students at institution: 21,574

Total number of mature students: 16,780

Mature Students' Officer

Phone: 01443 483541

Applications

General entry qualifications that are considered acceptable for mature applicants without the normal standard entry qualifications:

Access Course	Yes
APEL/APL	Yes

The institution does not interview all mature applicants.

Funding

There are specific mature student bursaries available over and above the national funds.

Study

Negotiated flexible learning is available on most courses.
It is available to:

Full-time students	Perhaps
Part-time students	Yes
Distance Learning students	Yes

Timetabling hours

Lectures are timetabled between 9am and 9pm.
Modules can be studied that require attending only morning lectures.

Accommodation and childcare

Accommodation is available:
Specifically for mature students No – but students can be placed in
'quieter' accommodation on request. For mature students with families Yes
– while all accommodation on campus is single occupancy, there are private
sector houses suitable for families. Accommodation Services will help in
this search.
The institution does have crèche/childcare facilities.
There are 60 spaces.
Spaces are not always available.
A holiday playcare scheme operates for an additional 40 children.

University of Glasgow

University Avenue
Glasgow
G12 8QQ
Phone: 0141 339 8855
Website: www.gla.ac.uk
Total number of students at institution: 23,328
Total number of mature students: 9,025

Mature Students' Officer

Irene Vezza
Phone: 0141 330 1823
Fax: 0141 330 1821
Email: i.vezza@educ.gla.ac.uk

Student Support Services

Phone: 0141 330 2850

Fax: 0141 330 3141

Student Counselling/Advisory

Phone: 0141 330 4528

Fax: 0141 330 3743

Applications

General entry qualifications that are considered acceptable for mature applicants without the normal standard entry qualifications:

Access Course	Yes
Essay submission	No
Entrance exam	No
APEL/APL	No

The institution does not interview all mature applicants.

Funding

There are specific mature student bursaries available over and above the national funds.

Study

Negotiated flexible learning is available on most courses.

It is available to:

Full-time students	Yes
Part-time students	Yes
Distance Learning students	Yes

Timetabling hours

Lectures are timetabled between 9am and 6pm.

Modules can be studied that require attending only morning lectures.

Accommodation and childcare

Accommodation is available:

Specifically for mature students	Yes – postgraduate accommodation/ mature students'

	accommodation in single room in 3-5 person flats
For mature students with families	Yes – a number of self-contained flats both owned and managed by the university

The institution does have crèche/childcare facilities.
There are 74 spaces.
Spaces are not always available.

General
The mature students' society organises social activities for mature students.
There is online information specifically for mature students at
www.gla.ac.uk/homepages/maturestudents/

Glasgow Caledonian University
Cowcaddens Road
Glasgow
G4 0BA
Phone: 0800 027 9171
Fax: 0141 331 3005
Email: helpline@gcal.ac.uk
Website: www.caledonian.ac.uk

Student Funding Manager
Sue Hindhaugh
Phone: 0141 331 3873
Email: funding@gcal.ac.uk

Applications
General entry qualifications that are considered acceptable for mature
applicants without the normal standard entry qualifications are dependent
on the individual programme. Please contact the institution for further
information.
The institution does not interview all mature applicants.

Funding
There are no specific mature student bursaries available over and above the national funds.

Study
Negotiated flexible learning is available on certain courses. Please contact the institution for further details.

Timetabling hours
Lecture times vary.

Accommodation and childcare
Accommodation is available:

Specifically for mature students	No
For mature students with families	No

The institution does have crèche/childcare facilities.
Spaces are not always available.
Please contact the institution for further details.

General
There are societies or organised social activities for mature students.
The main website contains useful information for mature students.
The university publishes a mature student guide that contains advice and guidance for mature applicants. Please contact the institution for further information.

University of Gloucestershire
PO Box 220
Park Campus
Cheltenham
GL50 2QE
Phone: 01242 532879
Fax: 01242 532810
Website: www.glos.ac.uk
Total number of students at institution: 9,700

Student Support Officer

Mary Moxham
Phone: 01242 532820
Email: mmoxham@glos.ac.uk

Applications

General entry qualifications that are considered acceptable for mature
applicants without the normal standard entry qualifications:

Access Course	Yes
Essay submission	No
Entrance exam	No
APEL/APL	Yes

The institution does not interview all mature applicants.

Study

Negotiated flexible learning is only available to distance learning students.

Timetabling hours

Lectures are timetabled between 9.15am and 9.15pm.
Modules can be studied that require attending only morning lectures.

Accommodation and childcare

Accommodation is available:

Specifically for mature students	No
For mature students with families	No

The institution does not have crèche/childcare facilities.

General

There are no societies or organised social activities for mature students.

Goldsmiths College

New Cross
London
SE14 6NW
Phone: 020 7919 7766
Fax: 020 7717 2240

Email: admissions@gold.ac.uk

Website: www.goldsmiths.ac.uk

Total number of students at institution: 9,071 (5,255 undergraduate)

Total number of undergraduate mature students: 2,652 (51 per cent)

Student Support Officer

Helen McNeely

Phone: 020 7919 7075

Fax: 020 7919 7241

Email: student-supp@gold.ac.uk

Applications

General entry qualifications that are considered acceptable for mature applicants without the normal standard entry qualifications:

Access Course	Yes
Essay submission	No
Entrance exam	Yes
APEL/APL	Yes
Other	Foundation certificate course.

The institution does interview most mature applicants.

Funding

There are no specific mature student bursaries available over and above the national funds.

Timetabling hours

Lecture times vary.

It may be possible that modules are studied that require attending only morning lectures, but this depends on the course.

Accommodation and childcare

Accommodation is available:

Specifically for mature students	Yes – self-catering accommodation on campus at approximately £70 per week.
For mature students with families	No

The institution does have crèche/childcare facilities, which are available for children aged between three months and five years.
There are 20 spaces.
Spaces are not always available.

General
There are no societies or organised social activities for mature students.
See www.gcsu.org.uk for details of all the college's societies.
There is online information specifically for mature students at www.goldsmiths.ac.uk/student-info/mature.php
Visit www.goldsmiths.ac.uk for details on Access and foundation certificate courses.

Great Yarmouth College
Southtown
Great Yarmouth
Norfolk
NR31 0ED
Phone: 01493 655261
Fax: 01493 653423
Email: info@gyc.ac.uk
Website: www.gyc.ac.uk
Total number of HE students at institution: 90
Total number of HE mature students: 20

Student Support Officer
Mrs A. Hodgson
Phone: 01493 419215
Fax: 01493 653423
Email: a.hodgson@gyc.ac.uk

Applications
General entry qualifications that are considered acceptable for mature applicants without the normal standard entry qualifications:

Access Course	Yes
Entrance exam	Yes
Other	Audition, portfolio of artwork.

The institution does interview all mature applicants.

Funding
There are no specific mature student bursaries available over and above the national funds.

Study
Negotiated flexible learning is not available on most courses.

Timetabling hours
Lecture times vary according to course.
Modules can be studied that require attending only morning lectures but this varies according to course.

Accommodation and childcare
Accommodation is available:

Specifically for mature students	No
For mature students with families	No

The institution does have crèche/childcare facilities.
Spaces are not always available.

General
There are no societies or organised social activities for mature students.
The institution is an FE college with some HE provision.

University of Greenwich
Maritime Greenwich Campus
Old Royal Naval College
Park Row
London
SE10 9LS
Phone: 0800 005 006
Fax: 020 8331 8145
Email: courseinfo@gre.ac.uk
Website: www.gre.ac.uk
Total number of students at institution: 16,066
Total number of mature students: 5,567

Student Support Officer

Phone: 020 8331 7868/9444

Fax: 020 8331 9478

Applications

General entry qualifications that are considered acceptable for mature applicants without the normal standard entry qualifications:

Access Course	Yes
Essay submission	No
Entrance exam	No
APEL/APL	Yes

The institution does not interview all mature applicants.

Funding

There are no specific mature student bursaries available over and above the national funds.

Study

Negotiated flexible learning is available on some courses.
It is available to:

Full-time students	No
Part-time students	Yes
Distance Learning students	Yes

Timetabling hours

Lectures are timetabled between 9am and 9pm, depending on the course.

Accommodation and childcare

Accommodation is available:

Specifically for mature students	Yes – Davenport House has 124 en-suite rooms available.
For mature students with families	No

The institution does have crèche/childcare facilities.
There are 30 spaces.
Spaces are not always available.

General
There are no societies or organised social activities for mature students.

Guildford College
Stoke Park
Guildford
Surrey
GU1 1EZ
Phone: 01483 448500
Fax: 01483 448600
Email: info@guildford.ac.uk
Website: www.guildford.ac.uk

Welfare Department
Phone: 01483 448560

Applications
General entry qualifications that are considered acceptable for mature applicants without the normal standard entry qualifications:
Other Proof of previous experience and a guidance interview.
The institution does not interview all mature applicants.

Funding
There are no specific mature student bursaries available over and above the national funds.

Study
Negotiated flexible learning is available on most courses.
It is available to:

Full-time students	No
Part-time students	Yes
Distance Learning students	Yes
Other	Some e-learning courses are available.

Timetabling hours
Lectures are timetabled between 9.30am and 8.00pm.
Modules can be studied that require attending only morning lectures.

Accommodation and childcare

Accommodation is available:

Specifically for mature students	No
For mature students with families	No

The institution does not have crèche/childcare facilities. However, it does have links with a local crèche with an allocated number of spaces for Guildford College students.

General

There are societies or organised social activities for mature students.

Halton College

Kingsway
Widnes
Cheshire
WA2 0QA
Phone: 0151 257 2020
Fax: 0151 420 2408
Email: studentservices@haltoncollege.ac.uk
Website: www.haltoncollege.ac.uk
Total number of students at institution: 344
Total number of mature students: 344

Welfare Office

Phone: 0151 257 2020

Applications

General entry qualifications that are considered acceptable for mature applicants without the normal standard entry qualifications:

Access Course	Yes
Essay submission	No
Entrance exam	No
APEL/APL	Yes

The institution does interview all mature applicants.

Funding
There are no specific mature student bursaries available over and above the national funds.

Study
Negotiated flexible learning is available to distance learning students only.

Timetabling hours
Lectures are timetabled between 9am and 9pm.
Modules can be studied that require attending only morning lectures.

Accommodation and childcare
Accommodation is available:

Specifically for mature students	No
For mature students with families	No

The institution does not have crèche/childcare facilities.

General
There are societies or organised social activities for all students, but not specifically for mature students.
There is general online information available, but not specifically for mature students.

Coleg Harlech
Harlech
Gwynedd
LL46 2PU
Phone: 01766 781900
Fax: 01766 780169
Email: info@harlech.ac.uk
Website: www.harlech.ac.uk
Total number of students at institution: 100
Total number of mature students: 100

Mature Students' Officer
Debbie Gardner
Phone: 01766 781900
Fax: 01766 780169
Email: info@harlech.ac.uk

Applications
Students do not need to have any prior qualification.
The institution does interview all mature applicants.

Funding
There are specific mature student bursaries available over and above the national funds.

Study
Negotiated flexible learning is not available on most courses.

Timetabling hours
Lectures are timetabled between 9am and 5pm.

Accommodation and childcare
Accommodation is available:

Specifically for mature students	Yes – halls of residence.
For mature students with families	No

The institution does not have crèche/childcare facilities.

General
There is online information specifically for mature students.
Coleg Harlech is an adult residential college providing Access courses in IT, performing and visual arts, social studies and Access to nursery.

Harper Adams University College
Edgmond
Newport
Shropshire
TF10 8NB
Phone: 01952 820280
Fax: 01952 814783
Website: www.harper-adams.ac.uk
Total number of students at institution: 1,800
Total number of mature students: 30

Student Support Officer
Bryony Allsop
Phone: 01952 815222

Fax: 01952 815222

Email: bryonyallsop@harper-adams.ac.uk

Applications

General entry qualifications that are considered acceptable for mature
applicants without the normal standard entry qualifications:

Other	Relevant experience.

The institution does interview all mature applicants.

Funding

There are no specific mature student bursaries available over and above the
national funds.

Study

Negotiated flexible learning is available on most courses.
It is available to:

Full-time students	Yes
Part-time students	Yes
Distance Learning students	No

Timetabling hours

Lectures are timetabled between 9am and 5pm.

Accommodation and childcare

Accommodation is available:

Specifically for mature students	Yes – limited self-catering accommodation in the locality.
For mature students with families	Yes – limited self-catering accommodation in the locality.

The institution does not have crèche/childcare facilities but has information
on local facilities.

General

There are societies or organised social activities for mature students. All students are members of the Students' Union and have access to the wide cross-section of activities provided.

Harris Manchester College

Mansfield Road
Oxford
OX1 3TD
Phone: 01865 271006
Fax: 01865 271012
Email: enquiries@hmc.ox.ac.uk
Website: www.hmc.ox.ac.uk
Total number of students at institution: 130
Total number of mature students: 130

Applications

General entry qualifications that are considered acceptable for mature applicants without the normal standard entry qualifications:

Access Course	Yes
Essay submission	No
Entrance exam	Yes
APEL/APL	No

The institution does not interview all mature applicants.

Funding

There are no specific mature student bursaries available over and above the national funds.

Study

Negotiated flexible learning is not available on most courses.

Timetabling hours

Lectures are timetabled between 9.00am and 9.00pm.
Modules cannot be studied that require attending only morning lectures.

Accommodation and childcare

Accommodation is available:

Specifically for mature students	Yes
For mature students with families	No – however, the University of Oxford can provide such accommodation

The institution does have crèche/childcare facilities. Spaces are not always available.

General

There are societies or organised social activities for mature students. As a mature students' college, all societies and social events are for them.

There is online information specifically for mature students at www.hmc.ox.ac.uk

Harris Manchester College is a college for mature students only (21 years and over).

Herefordshire College of Technology

Folly Lane
Hereford
HR1 1LS
Phone: 01432 352235
Fax: 01432 365357
Email: enquiries@herefordtech.co.uk
Website: www.herefordtech.co.uk

Student Support Officer

John Rogers
Phone: 01432 352235 ext. 258
Email: rogersj@herefordtech.co.uk

Applications

General entry qualifications that are considered acceptable for mature applicants without the normal standard entry qualifications:

APEL/APL	Yes
Other	Applications are considered individually.

The institution does interview all applicants, mature or otherwise.

Funding
There are no specific mature student bursaries available over and above the national funds.

Study
Negotiated flexible learning is not available on most courses.

Timetabling hours
Lectures are timetabled between 9am and 5pm. Evening classes also run.

Accommodation and childcare
Accommodation is available:

Specifically for mature students	No
For mature students with families	No

The institution does have crèche/childcare facilities.

There are 50 spaces.

Spaces are not always available.

General
There are no societies or organised social activities for mature students.

Heriot Watt University
Riccarton
Edinburgh
EH14 4AS
Phone: 0131 449 5111
Fax: 0131 449 5153
Email: enquiries@hw.ac.uk
Website: www.hw.ac.uk
Total number of students at institution: 5,500

Student Counsellor
Morag Patten
Phone: 0131 451 3387
Email: m.i.patten@hw.ac.uk

Applications
General entry qualifications that are considered acceptable for mature applicants without the normal standard entry qualifications:

Access Course	Yes
Essay submission	No
Entrance exam	No
APEL/APL	Yes
Other	Mature students are advised to contact the University to speak to an admissions tutor before applying.

The institution does not interview all mature applicants, but they are encouraged to visit the University.

Funding
There are no specific mature student bursaries available over and above the national funds.

Study
Negotiated flexible learning is not available on most courses.
It is available to:

Full-time students	No
Part-time students	No
Distance Learning students	Yes

Timetabling hours
Lectures are timetabled between 9.00am and 5.00pm.
Modules cannot be studied that require attending only morning lectures.

Accommodation and childcare
Accommodation is available:

Specifically for mature students	No
For mature students with families	Yes – for married couples.

The institution does have crèche/childcare facilities.
Spaces are always available.

General
There are societies or organised social activities for mature students. The Students' Association has a mature students' representative.

University of Hertfordshire
Hatfield Campus
College Lane
Hatfield
Hertfordshire
AL10 9AB
Phone: 01707 284000
Fax: 01707 284115
Website: www.herts.ac.uk

Student Finance Officer
Sandie Cranfield
Phone: 01707 284464
Email: s.cranfield@herts.ac.uk

Applications
General entry qualifications that are considered acceptable for mature applicants without the normal standard entry qualifications:

Access Course	Yes
APEL/APL	Yes
Other	Essay, exam and interview on individual case basis.

The institution does not interview all mature applicants.

Funding
There are specific mature student bursaries available over and above the national funds: hardship funds.

Study
Negotiated flexible learning is available on most courses.
It is available to:

Full-time students	Yes
Part-time students	Yes
Distance Learning students	No

Timetabling hours

Lectures are timetabled between 9am and 6pm.

Modules cannot be studied that require attending only morning lectures.

Accommodation and childcare

Accommodation is available:

Specifically for mature students	No
For mature students with families	No

The institution does have crèche/childcare facilities.

There are 47 spaces.

There is a 50 weeks in the year provision for 0–5 year olds. There is a waiting list for places.

General

There are societies or organised social activities for mature students. The Students' Union provides a society if there is sufficient interest.

Heythrop College

Kensington Square
London
W8 5HQ
Phone: 020 7795 6600
Fax: 020 7795 4200
Email: enquiries@heythrop.ac.uk
Website: www.heythrop.ac.uk
Total number of students at institution: 550
Total number of mature students: 440

Student Support Officer

The Chaplain
Phone: 020 7795 6600
Fax: 020 7795 4200
Email: enquiries@heythrop.ac.uk

Applications

General entry qualifications that are considered acceptable for mature applicants without the normal standard entry qualifications:

Access Course	Yes

The institution does interview all mature applicants.

Funding

There are no specific mature student bursaries available over and above the national funds.

Study

Negotiated flexible learning is not available on most courses.

Timetabling hours

Lectures are timetabled between 10am and 8.30pm.
Modules can be studied that require attending only morning lectures.

Accommodation and childcare

Accommodation is available:

Specifically for mature students	No
For mature students with families	No

The institution does have crèche/childcare facilities.
The facilities are not on campus.

General

There are no societies or organised social activities for mature students.
There is no online information specifically for mature students.

Homerton College

Hills Road
Cambridge
CB2 2PH
Phone: 01223 507252
Fax: 01223 507206
Email: admissions@homerton.cam.ac.uk
Website: www.homerton.cam.ac.uk

Total number of students at institution: 550
Total number of mature students: 38

Mature Students' Officer

Phone: 01223 507203
Fax: 01223 507206
Email: admissions@homerton.cam.ac.uk

Applications

General entry qualifications that are considered acceptable for mature applicants without the normal standard entry qualifications:

Access Course	Yes
Essay submission	No
Entrance exam	No
APEL/APL	No

The institution does interview all mature applicants.

Funding

There are specific mature student bursaries available over and above the national funds.

Study

Negotiated flexible learning is not available on most courses.

Timetabling hours

Lectures are timetabled between 9.00am and 6.00pm.
Modules cannot be studied that require attending only morning lectures.

Accommodation and childcare

Accommodation is available:

Specifically for mature students	No
For mature students with families	No

The institution does not have crèche/childcare facilities. However, there is online information at www.cam.ac.uk/cambuniv/childcare/childguide.

General

There are no societies or organised social activities for mature students.

Hopwood Hall College

Rochdale Road
Middleton
Manchester
M24 6XH
Phone: 0161 643 7560
Fax: 0161 643 2114
Email: enquiries@hopwood.ac.uk
Website: www.hopwood.ac.uk
Total number of students at institution: 10,000
Total number of mature students: 7,000 (300 full-time)

Student Support Officer

Ted Taylor
Phone: 0161 643 7560
Fax: 0161 643 2114
Email: ted.taylor@hopwood.ac.uk

Applications

General entry qualifications that are considered acceptable for mature applicants without the normal standard entry qualifications:

Access Course	Yes
Essay submission	No
Entrance exam	Yes
APEL/APL	Yes
Other	Portfolio for art and design courses.

The institution does interview all full-time and some part-time mature applicants.

Funding

There are no specific mature student bursaries available over and above the national funds.

Study

Negotiated flexible learning is not available on most courses.

Timetabling hours

Lectures are timetabled between 9.30am to 3pm (Access).

Modules can be studied that require attending only morning lectures.

Accommodation and childcare

Accommodation is available:

Specifically for mature students	Yes – halls of residence.
For mature students with families	Yes – Homestay.

The institution does have crèche/childcare facilities.

There are 60 spaces.

Spaces are not always available.

College crèches fill up quickly but you can use outside nurseries as back-up.

General

Access students organise group events for mature students.

University of Huddersfield

Queensgate
Huddersfield
West Yorkshire
HD1 3DH
Phone: 01484 422288
Email: prospectus@hud.ac.uk
Website: www.hud.ac.uk

Mature Students' Officer

Melanie Ritson
Email: stun-mature@hud.ac.uk

Students' Adviser

Charlotte Mutton
Phone: 01484 473446
Email: C.J.Mutton@hud.ac.uk

Applications

General entry qualifications that are considered acceptable for mature applicants without the normal standard entry qualifications:

Access Course	Yes
Essay submission	Yes
Entrance exam	Yes
APEL/APL	Yes

The institution does interview all mature applicants.

Funding

There are no specific mature student bursaries available over and above the national funds.

Study

Negotiated flexible learning is not available on most courses.

Timetabling hours

Modules cannot be studied that require attending only morning lectures.

Accommodation and childcare

Accommodation is available:

Specifically for mature students	Yes
For mature students with families	No

The institution does have crèche/childcare facilities.

There are 24 spaces.

Spaces are not always available.

General

There are societies or organised social activities for mature students.

There is no online information specifically for mature students.

A Mature Students' Handbook is available on request – please call 0870 901 5555 or email prospectus@hud.ac.uk

Hughes Hall

Cambridge

CB1 2EW

Phone: 01223 334898

Fax: 01223 311179

Email: Hughes@cam.ac.uk

Website: www.hughes.cam.ac.uk

Applications

General entry qualifications that are considered acceptable for mature applicants without the normal standard entry qualifications:

Access Course	Yes
Entrance exam	Yes

The institution does not interview all mature applicants.

Funding

There are no specific mature student bursaries available over and above the national funds.

Study

Negotiated flexible learning is not available on most courses.

Timetabling hours

Lectures are timetabled between 9am and 5pm Monday to Saturday. Modules cannot be studied that require attending only morning lectures.

Accommodation and childcare

Accommodation is available:

Specifically for mature students	Yes – for all students over 21.
For mature students with families	No

The institution does not have crèche/childcare facilities.

General

There are societies or organised social activities for mature students. The college MCR organises events throughout the year.
There is online information specifically for mature students at www.hughes.cam.ac.uk

---

University of Hull

Cottingham Road
Hull HU6 7RX
Phone: 01482 346311
Email: admissions@hull.ac.uk
Website: www.hull.ac.uk

Total number of students at institution: 9,300 (undergraduate)
Total number of mature students: 4,000 (undergraduate)

Mature Students' Officer

Phone: 01482 465033
Fax: 01482 465297
Email: k.smales@hull.ac.uk

Applications

General entry qualifications that are considered acceptable for mature
applicants without the normal standard entry qualifications:

Access Course	Yes
Essay submission	Yes
Entrance exam	Yes
APEL/APL	Yes

All of the above may apply, but each case is judged on individual merit.
The institution does not interview all mature applicants.

Funding

There are no specific mature student bursaries available over and above the
national funds.

Study

Negotiated flexible learning is only available to part-time students.

Timetabling hours

Lectures are timetabled between 9am and 6pm for full-time students.
Modules cannot be studied that require attending only morning lectures.

Accommodation and childcare

Accommodation is available:

Specifically for mature students	No
For mature students with families	No

The institution does have crèche/childcare facilities. The *Guardian*
newspaper has recently praised the quality of the institution's day nursery
childcare provision.
There are 49 equivalent full-time spaces.
Spaces are not always available.

General

The mature students' society organises social activities for mature students. There is online information specifically for mature students. Information can be accessed from the homepage (both the 'open days' and 'prospective students' links).

The institution says it welcomes mature students and recognises that their high degree of motivation and breadth of experience are valuable assets.

Imperial College London

South Kensington Campus
London
SW7 2AZ
Phone: 020 7589 5111
Fax: 020 7594 8004
Email: info@imperial.ac.uk
Website: www.imperial.ac.uk
Total number of students at institution: 11,313

Applications

General entry qualifications that are considered acceptable for mature applicants without the normal standard entry qualifications:

Access Course	No
Essay submission	No
Entrance exam	No
APEL/APL	No

The institution does not interview all mature applicants.

Funding

There are no specific mature student bursaries available over and above the national funds.

Study

Negotiated flexible learning is not available on most courses.

Timetabling hours

Lectures are timetabled between 9am and 5.50pm except Wednesdays, when they are between 9am and 12.30pm.
Modules cannot be studied that require attending only morning lectures.

Accommodation and childcare

Accommodation is available:

Specifically for mature students	No
For mature students with families	No

The institution does have crèche/childcare facilities.
There are 54 spaces.
Spaces are not always available.

General

There are no societies or organised social activities for mature students.

Isle of Man College

Homefield Road
Douglas
Isle of Man
IM2 6RB
Phone: 01624 648200
Fax: 01624 648201
Email: enquiries@iomcollege.ac.im
Website: www.iomcollege.ac.im
Total number of students at institution: 9,000
Total number of mature students: 5,000

Mature Students' Officer

Ian Sheard
Phone: 01624 648220
Fax: 01624 648201
Email: ian.sheard@iomcollege.ac.im

Student Support Officer

Anne Gundry
Phone: 01624 648221
Fax: 01624 648201
Email: anne.gundry@iomcollege.ac.im

Applications

General entry qualifications that are considered acceptable for mature
applicants without the normal standard entry qualifications:

Access Course	Yes
Essay submission	No
Entrance exam	No
APEL/APL	Yes

The institution does interview all mature applicants.

Funding

There are no specific mature student bursaries available over and above the national funds.

Study

Negotiated flexible learning is available on most courses.
It is available to:

Full-time students	Yes
Part-time students	Yes

Timetabling hours

Lectures are timetabled between 9am and 9pm.
Modules can be studied that require attending only morning lectures.

Accommodation and childcare

Accommodation is available:

Specifically for mature students	No
For mature students with families	No

The institution does have crèche/childcare facilities.
There are 25 spaces.
Spaces are not always available.

General

There are societies or organised social activities for mature students.
These are organised by the IOM Higher Education Students' Forum.
There is online information specifically for mature students.

Keele University

Keele
Staffordshire ST5 5BG
Phone: 01782 621111
Fax: 01782 632343

Email: aaa26@keele.ac.uk
Website: www.keele.ac.uk
Total number of mature students: 15 per cent of the total student body

Mature Students' Officer

Phone: 01782 583700
Fax: 01782 712671
Email: sta21@keele.ac.uk

Student Support Officer

Mr R. Hughes
Phone: 01782 583912
Fax: 01782 583998
Email: aaa64@keele.ac.uk

Applications

General entry qualifications that are considered acceptable for mature
applicants without the normal standard entry qualifications:

Access Course	Yes
Essay submission	Yes
Entrance exam	No
APEL/APL	Yes
Other	One A-level qualification.

The institution does not interview all mature applicants.

Funding

There are specific mature student bursaries available over and above the
national funds.

Study

Negotiated flexible learning is available on some courses.
It is available to:

Full-time students	Yes
Part-time students	No
Distance Learning students	No
Other	Postgraduate level only for part-time and distance learning students.

Timetabling hours

Lectures are timetabled between 9am and 7pm.

Modules can be studied that require attending only morning lectures.

Accommodation and childcare

Accommodation is available:

Specifically for mature students	No
For mature students with families	Yes

The institution does have crèche/childcare facilities.

There is a restriction on numbers.

General

There are societies or organised social activities for mature students.

There is online information specifically for mature students at www.keele.ac.uk/undergraduate/about/mature.htm.

University of Kent

Canterbury

Kent CT2 7NZ

Phone: 01227 764000

Website: www.kent.ac.uk

Total number of students at institution: 13,029

Total number of mature students: 6,044

Mature Students' Officer

Phone: 01227 824200

Fax: 01227 824204

Email: union@kent.ac.uk

Welfare Officer

Phone: 01227 824200

Fax: 01227 824204

Email: union@kent.ac.uk

Applications

General entry qualifications that are considered acceptable for mature applicants without the normal standard entry qualifications:

Access Course	Yes
Essay submission	Yes
Entrance exam	No
APEL/APL	Yes

The institution does not interview all mature applicants.

Funding
There are no specific mature student bursaries available over and above the national funds.

Study
Negotiated flexible learning is available on most courses.

Timetabling hours
Lectures are timetabled between 9.00am and 9.30pm.

Accommodation and childcare
Accommodation is available:

Specifically for mature students	Yes
For mature students with families	No

The institution does have crèche/childcare facilities.

General
There are societies or organised social activities for mature students.
There is online information specifically for mature students at www.kent.ac.uk/url/.

Kent Institute of Art and Design
Oakwood Park
Maidstone
ME16 8AG
Phone: 01622 757286
Fax: 01622 621100
Website: www.kiad.ac.uk
Total number of students at institution: 2,878

Student Support Officer

Judy Keay
Phone: 01227 769371
Fax: 01227 877500
Email: JKeay@kiad.ac.uk

Applications

General entry qualifications that are considered acceptable for mature applicants without the normal standard entry qualifications:

Access Course	Yes
Essay submission	No
Entrance exam	No
APEL/APL	No
Other	Portfolio and experience.

The institution does not interview all mature applicants.

Funding

There are no specific mature student bursaries available over and above the national funds.

Study

Negotiated flexible learning is not available on most courses.

Timetabling hours

Lectures are timetabled between 9.00am and 9.00pm.

Accommodation and childcare

Accommodation is available:

Specifically for mature students	No
For mature students with families	No

The institution does not have crèche/childcare facilities.

General

There are no societies or organised social activities for mature students. There is online information specifically for mature students regarding how to apply with links to potential courses.

King Alfred's College
Winchester
Hampshire
SO22 4NR
Phone: 01962 841515
Fax: 01962 842280
Email: admissions@wkac.ac.uk
Website: www.kingalfreds.ac.uk

Welfare Officer
Phone: 01962 827341
Fax: 01962 842280
Email: welfare@wkac.ac.uk

Applications
General entry qualifications that are considered acceptable for mature
applicants without the normal standard entry qualifications:

Access Course	Yes
Essay submission	No
Entrance exam	No
APEL/APL	Yes
Other	Non-standard entry is adjudicated by registrar.

The institution does not interview all mature applicants.

Funding
There are specific mature student bursaries available over and above the
national funds.

Study
Negotiated flexible learning is available on most courses.
It is available to:

Full-time students	Yes
Part-time students	Yes
Distance Learning students	No

Timetabling hours

Lectures are timetabled between 9am and 6pm.

Modules can be studied that require attending only morning lectures.

Accommodation and childcare

Accommodation is available:

Specifically for mature students	Yes – mature students' flats.
For mature students with families	No

The institution does have crèche/childcare facilities.

Spaces are not always available.

General

There are societies or organised social activities for mature students.

Mature students report and get together on induction.

King's College London

Strand

London

WC2R 2LS

Phone: 020 7836 5454

Website: www.kcl.ac.uk

Total number of students at institution: 18,000

Applications

General entry qualifications that are considered acceptable for mature applicants without the normal standard entry qualifications:

Access Course	No
Essay submission	No

The institution does not interview all mature applicants.

Funding

There are no specific mature student bursaries available over and above the national funds.

Study

Negotiated flexible learning is available on most courses.
It is available to:

Full-time students	Yes
Part-time students	Yes

Timetabling hours

Lectures are timetabled between 9am and 6pm.
Modules can be studied that require attending only morning lectures.

Accommodation and childcare

Accommodation is available:

Specifically for mature students	No – there is one small hall for postgraduates.
For mature students with families	No

The institution does not have crèche/childcare facilities.

General

There are societies or organised social activities for mature students. There is a postgraduate society which all can join.
There is no online information specifically for mature students.

Laban

Creekside
London
SE8 3DZ
Phone: 020 8691 8600
Fax: 020 8691 8400
Email: info@laban.org
Website: www.laban.org
Total number of students at institution: 340
Total number of mature students: 40

Applications

Entry requirements depend on the course applied for.

The institution auditions all mature applicants where applicable; some courses are purely application-based.

Funding

There are no specific mature student bursaries available over and above the national funds.

Study

Negotiated flexible learning is not available on most courses.

Timetabling hours

Lecture times vary.

Modules cannot be studied that require attending only morning lectures.

Accommodation and childcare

Accommodation is available:

Specifically for mature students	No
For mature students with families	No

The institution does not have crèche/childcare facilities.

General

There are no societies or organised social activities for mature students.

There is no online information specifically for mature students.

Lakes College West Cumbria

Hallwood Road
Lillyhall Business Park
Lillyhall
Workington
Cumbria
CA14 4JN
Phone: 01946 839300
Fax: 01946 839302
Email: info@lcwc.ac.uk
Website: www.lcwc.ac.uk
Total number of mature students: c. 60 per cent of the students are aged 21+

Head of Student Support
Maggie Szuster
Phone: 01946 839300
Email: Maggie.szuster@lwcw.ac.uk

Applications
General entry qualifications that are considered acceptable for mature
applicants without the normal standard entry qualifications:

Access Course	Yes
Essay submission	No
Entrance exam	No
APEL/APL	Yes
Other	Experience is taken into account.

The institution does interview all mature applicants.

Funding
There are no specific mature student bursaries available over and above the
national funds.

Study
Negotiated flexible learning is not available on most courses.

Timetabling hours
Lectures are timetabled between 9am and 9pm.
Modules can be studied that require attending only morning lectures.

Accommodation and childcare
Accommodation is available:

Specifically for mature students	No
For mature students with families	No

The institution does not have crèche/childcare facilities.
The college has plans to open a crèche.

General
There are no societies or organised social activities specifically for mature
students, but they are welcome to join the students' association.

Lancaster University
Bailrigg
Lancaster
LA1 4YW
Phone: 01524 65201
Fax: 01542 846243
Email: ugadmissions@lancaster.ac.uk
Website: www.lancs.ac.uk
Total number of students at institution: 7,000
Total number of mature students: 525–700

Mature Students' Officer
Phone: 01524 594291
Fax: 01524 594294
Email: studentsupport@lancs.ac.uk

Applications
General entry qualifications that are considered acceptable for mature applicants without the normal standard entry qualifications:

Access Course	Yes
Other	Students are considered on an individual basis.

The institution does not interview all mature applicants.

Funding
There are specific mature student bursaries available over and above the national funds. See www.lancs.ac.uk/users/studentsupport/scholarships for details.

Study
Negotiated flexible learning is not available on most courses.

Timetabling hours
Lectures are timetabled between 9am and 5pm.
Modules cannot be studied that require attending only morning lectures.

Accommodation and childcare
Accommodation is available:

Specifically for mature students	Yes – see www.lancs.ac.uk/users/cro/contents
For mature students with families	Yes – there are campus flats and help in finding private housing is available: see website.

The institution does have crèche/childcare facilities.
There are 120+ spaces.
Spaces are not always available.
See www.lancs.ac.uk/depts/pre-school

General

There are societies or organised social activities for mature students. These are organised by the students' union mature students' representative.
There is online information specifically for mature students at www.lancs.ac.uk/users/studentsupport/mature.
A mature student guide is issued to applicants through admissions.

Lancaster and Morecambe College

Morecambe Road
Lancaster
LA1 2TY
Phone: 0800 306306
Fax: 01524 843078
Email: info@lanmore.ac.uk
Website: www.lanmore.ac.uk
Total number of students at institution: 12,000
Total number of mature students: 7,000

Student Services

Phone: 01524 521237
Fax: 01524 843078
Email: info@lanmore.ac.uk

Applications

General entry qualifications that are considered acceptable for mature applicants without the normal standard entry qualifications:

Access Course	Yes
Essay submission	No
Entrance exam	No
APEL/APL	Yes
Other	Personal interview

The institution interviews all applicants for full-time courses. Most applicants for part-time courses do not require an interview.

Funding

There are no specific mature student bursaries available over and above the national funds.

Study

Negotiated flexible learning is not available on most courses.
It is available to:

Full-time students	No
Part-time students	No
Distance Learning students	Yes

Timetabling hours

Lectures are timetabled between 9.00am and 4.30pm.
Modules cannot be studied that require attending only morning lectures.

Accommodation and childcare

Accommodation is available:

Specifically for mature students	No
For mature students with families	No

The institution does have crèche/childcare facilities.
There are 30 spaces.
Spaces are not always available.

General

There are no societies or organised social activities for mature students.

Leeds College of Art and Design

Blenheim Walk
Leeds
LS2 9AQ
Phone: 0113 202 8000
Fax: 0113 202 8001
Email: info@leeds-art.ac.uk
Website: www.leeds-art.ac.uk

Mature Students' Officer

Phone: 0113 202 8000
Fax: 0113 202 8001
Email: info@leeds-art.ac.uk

Applications

General entry qualifications that are considered acceptable for mature
applicants without the normal standard entry qualifications:

Access Course	Yes
Essay submission	No
Entrance exam	No
APEL/APL	Yes

The institution does interview all mature applicants.

Funding

There are no specific mature student bursaries available over and above the
national funds.

Study

Negotiated flexible learning is not available on most courses.

Timetabling hours

Lectures are timetabled between 9am and 4pm.
Modules can be studied that require attending only morning lectures.

Accommodation and childcare

Accommodation is available:

Specifically for mature students	No
For mature students with families	No

The institution does not have crèche/childcare facilities.

General

There are no societies or organised social activities for mature students.

Leeds Metropolitan University

City Campus
Leeds
Phone: 0113 283 3113
Fax: 0113 283 5906
Email: course-enquiries@lmu.ac.uk
Website: www.lmu.ac.uk

Student Services

Phone: 0113 283 3115
Fax: 0113 283 3063
Website: www.lmu.ac.uk

Applications

General entry qualifications that are considered acceptable for mature applicants without the normal standard entry qualifications:

Access Course	Yes
APEL/APL	Yes

The institution does not interview all mature applicants.

Funding

There are no specific mature student bursaries available over and above the national funds.

Study

Negotiated flexible learning is available on some part-time courses. Individual programmes of study are offered in most areas, e.g. business, social science, and health studies.

Timetabling hours

Lectures are timetabled between 9am and 9pm.
Modules cannot be studied that require attending only morning lectures.

Accommodation and childcare

Accommodation is available:

Specifically for mature students	No
For mature students with families	No

The institution does have crèche/childcare facilities. Leeds City Council childcare facilities are used.
Spaces are not always available.

General

There is no online information specifically for mature students.

University of Leicester

University Road
Leicester LE1 7RH
Phone: 0116 252 2522
Fax: 0116 252 2200
Email: admissions@le.ac.uk
Website: www.le.ac.uk
Total number of undergraduate students at institution: 8,000
Total number of mature students: 800 (i.e. 10 per cent)

Mature Students' Officer

Phone: 0116 223 1111
Fax: 0116 252 2447
Email: jb74@le.ac.uk

Student Welfare Service

Phone: 0116 223 1185
Email: welfare@le.ac.uk

Applications

General entry qualifications that are considered acceptable for mature applicants without the normal standard entry qualifications:

Access Course	Yes
Essay Submission	No
Entrance exam	No

Other	Each case is considered on merit.

The institution does not interview all mature applicants.

Funding

There are specific mature student bursaries available over and above the national funds.

Study

Negotiated flexible learning is not available on most courses.
It is available to:

Full-time students	No
Part-time students	No
Distance Learning students	Yes

Timetabling hours

Lectures are timetabled between 8.30am and 6.30pm.
Modules cannot be studied that require attending only morning lectures.

Accommodation and childcare

Accommodation is available:

Specifically for mature students	Yes – available through University accommodation service.
For mature students with families	Yes – available through University accommodation service.

The institution does not have crèche/childcare facilities. However, information is held about local childcare and schools.

General

There are societies or organised social activities for mature students.
There is online information specifically for mature students available through the main website www.le.ac.uk

For pre-entry financial and academic advice telephone Jean Baxter, Assistant Registrar for Widening Participation, on 0116 223 1381.

University of Lincoln
Brayford Pool
Lincoln LN6 7TS
Phone: 01522 882000
Fax: 01522 882088
Email: enquiries@lincoln.ac.uk
Website: www.lincoln.ac.uk

Student Support Officer
Judith Carey
Phone: 01522 886016
Email: jcarey@lincoln.ac.uk

Applications
General entry qualifications that are considered acceptable for mature applicants without the normal standard entry qualifications:

Access Course	Yes
APEL/APL	Yes
Other Experience in programme area.	

The institution does not interview all mature applicants.

Funding
There are specific mature student bursaries available over and above the national funds.

Timetabling hours
Lectures are timetabled between 9am and 6pm.
Modules cannot be studied that require attending only morning lectures.

Accommodation and childcare
Accommodation is available:

Specifically for mature students	No
For mature students with families	No

The institution does not have crèche/childcare facilities.

General

There are no societies or organised social activities for mature students.
There is online information specifically for mature students.
The university has its own mature students' guide, available on request.

University of Liverpool

Liverpool
L69 3BX
Phone: 0151 794 2000
Website: www.liv.ac.uk

Mature Students' Contact Address

Centre for Lifelong Learning
Widening Participation
Sir Alistair Pilkington Building
Mulberry Street
Liverpool
L69 7SH
Email: uksro@liv.ac.uk
Total number of full-time undergraduate students at institution: 14,193
Total number of mature students: unknown, but there are 5,194 part-time
undergraduate students

Mature Students' Officer

Phone: 0151 794 1319
Fax: 0151 794 1310
Email: a.davies@liv.ac.uk

Applications

General entry qualifications that are considered acceptable for mature
applicants without the normal standard entry qualifications:

Access Course	Yes
Essay submission	Yes – may be applicable: some degrees that have foundation years (2+2) are available without formal qualifications.

Entrance exam	No
APEL/APL	Yes – may be applicable: some degrees that have foundation years (2+2) are available without formal qualifications.

The institution does not interview all mature applicants, but this depends on the department; some run specific open/interview days just for mature students.

Funding
There are specific mature student bursaries available over and above the national funds.

Study
Negotiated flexible learning is not available on most courses. However, there is some flexibility in module choice for part-time students.

Timetabling hours
Lectures are timetabled between 9am and 5pm, but there is some evening provision until 9pm.
Depending on the course, some modules can be studied that require attending only morning lectures.

Accommodation and childcare
Accommodation is available:

Specifically for mature students	No – but the institution tries to ensure that all mature students are housed together.
For mature students with families	Yes – but this is limited to two children.

The institution does have crèche/childcare facilities.
There are 68 spaces.
Spaces are not always available.
Half-term and holiday play schemes are available.

General

There are societies or organised social activities for mature students.
These are organised by MatSoc – the mature students' society.
There is online information specifically for mature students.
Please use the mature students' adviser as the first point of contact for general enquiries.

Liverpool Institute for Performing Arts (LIPA)

Mount Street
Liverpool
L1 9HF
Phone: 0151 330 3000
Fax: 0151 330 3131
Email: reception@lipa.ac.uk
Website: www.lipa.ac.uk
Total number of students at institution: 650
Total number of mature students: 40

Student Welfare Services

(at Liverpool John Moores University)
Phone: 0151 231 3167

Applications

General entry qualifications that are considered acceptable for mature applicants without the normal standard entry qualifications:

Access Course	Yes
Other	Audition/interview.

All applicants are assessed against five criteria and additional experience is taken into account for mature students.
The institution does not automatically interview all mature applicants.

Funding

There are no specific mature student bursaries available over and above the national funds.

Study

Negotiated flexible learning is not available on most courses.

Timetabling hours

Lectures are timetabled between 9.00am and 7.00pm.
Modules cannot be studied that require attending only morning lectures.

Accommodation and childcare

LIPA does not have its own student accommodation but provides accommodation via partnership arrangements with private housing companies, which offer a range of accommodation popular with mature students.
The institution does have crèche/childcare facilities through Liverpool John Moores University.

General

There are no societies or organised social activities for mature students.
LIPA has a connected relationship with Liverpool John Moores University, which means all students can access a wide range of JMU welfare services.

Liverpool John Moores University

Roscoe Court
4 Rodney Street
Liverpool
L1 2TZ
Phone: 0151 231 5090
Fax: 0151 231 3462
Email: recruitment@livjm.ac.uk
Website: www.livjm.ac.uk
Total number of students at institution: 20,000

Student Support Officer

Helen Orme
Phone: 0151 231 3209
Fax: 0151 231 3462
Email: mkghorme@livjm.ac.uk

Applications

General entry qualifications that are considered acceptable for mature applicants without the normal standard entry qualifications:

Access Course	Yes
Essay submission	Yes
Entrance exam	Yes
APEL/APL	Yes
Other	Interview

The institution does not interview all mature applicants.

Funding

There are no specific mature student bursaries available over and above the national funds.

Study

Negotiated flexible learning is available on most courses.
It is available to:

Full-time students	No
Part-time students	Yes

Timetabling hours

Lectures are timetabled between 9am and 8pm, Monday to Friday.
Modules cannot be studied that require attending only morning lectures.

Accommodation and childcare

Accommodation is available:

Specifically for mature students	Yes – private halls /accommodation.
For mature students with families	Yes – private accommodation and some halls.

The institution does have crèche/childcare facilities.
Spaces are not always available.

General

There are societies or organised social activities for mature students.

These are organised by students' union societies.

The institution prides itself on being popular with mature students from a wide mix of backgrounds. Mature students are encouraged to apply.

University College London

Gower Street
London
WC1E 6BT
Phone: 020 7679 3000
Fax: 020 7679 3001
Website: www.ucl.ac.uk
Total number of students at institution: 18,300
Total number of mature students: 2,196 (i.e. 12 per cent)

Education and Welfare Officer

Phone: 020 7679 7930
Email: ew.officer@ucl.ac.uk

Applications

General entry qualifications that are considered acceptable for mature applicants without the normal standard entry qualifications:

Access Course	Yes
Other	Evidence of recent consistent academic study. Each case is considered individually.

The institution normally does interview all mature applicants.

Funding

There are no specific mature student bursaries available over and above the national funds.

Timetabling hours

Lectures are timetabled between 9.00am and 6.00pm.

Accommodation and childcare

Accommodation is available:

Specifically for mature students	No – however, accommodation application form allows students to specify a preference for sharing with mature and postgraduate students.
For mature students with families	Yes – there is some provision of accommodation for married students and those with families.

The institution does have crèche/childcare facilities.

There are 38 spaces.

There is normally a waiting list for places. For further information contact the Day Nursery on 020 7679 7461 or email nursery@ucl.ac.uk

General

There is online information specifically for mature students at www.ucl.ac.uk/prospective-students/applications-and-admissions

UCL welcomes mature students and each applicant is considered on an individual basis. Students should contact the appropriate admissions tutor with any specific queries about entry qualifications, study commitments or other matters.

University of London External Programme

Senate House
Malet Street
London
WC1E 7HN

Phone: 020 7862 8360
Fax: 020 7862 8358
Email: enquiries@lon.ac.uk
Website: www.londonexternal.ac.uk
Total number of students at institution: 30,000
Total number of mature students: 22,500

Applications

General entry qualifications that are considered acceptable for mature applicants without the normal standard entry qualifications:

Access Course	Yes
Essay submission	No
Entrance exam	No
Other	Special admissions for applicants aged over 21.

The institution does not interview all mature applicants.

Funding

There are no specific mature student bursaries available over and above the national funds.

Study

Negotiated flexible learning is available on most courses.
It is available to:

Full-time students	Yes
Part-time students	Yes
Distance Learning students	Yes
Other	All students manage their own study schemes.

Timetabling hours

Study is by distance learning.

Accommodation and childcare

Accommodation is available:

Specifically for mature students	No
For mature students with families	No

The institution does not have crèche/childcare facilities.

General

There are no societies or organised social activities for mature students. The external programme operates an informal student-to-student network, which is open to all registered students. This allows students to contact others studying for the same degree for initial support.

London Business School

Regent's Park
London
NW1 4SA
Phone: 020 7262 5050
Fax: 020 7724 7875
Website: www.london.edu
Total number of students at institution: c. 1,400 (all mature students)

Applications

General entry qualifications that are considered acceptable for mature applicants without the normal standard entry qualifications:
Other Cases are assessed on an individual basis.
The institution does interview all mature applicants.

Funding

There are no specific mature student bursaries available over and above the national funds.

Study

Negotiated flexible learning is not available on most courses.

Timetabling hours

Lecture times are varied.

General

The London Business School offers only postgraduate programmes, so all its students can be classed as mature.

London College of Fashion
20 John Prince's Street
London
W1G 0BJ
Phone: 020 7514 7344
Fax: 020 7514 8388
Email: enquiries@lcf.linst.ac.uk
Website: www.lcf.linst.ac.uk
Total number of students at institution: 3,500

Mature Students' Officer
Phone: 020 7514 7430
Fax: 020 7514 7415
Email: student.services@linst.ac.uk

Applications
General entry qualifications that are considered acceptable for mature applicants without the normal standard entry qualifications:

Access Course	Yes
Essay submission	No
Entrance exam	No
Other	Work experience.

Funding
There are specific mature student bursaries available over and above the national funds.

Study
Negotiated flexible learning is available to distance learning students.

Timetabling hours
Lecture times vary.
Modules cannot be studied that require attending only morning lectures.

Accommodation and childcare
Accommodation is available:

Specifically for mature students	No – email accommodation@ linst.ac.uk for assistance.

| For mature students with families | No – email student.services@ linst.ac.uk for assistance. |

The institution does have crèche/childcare facilities.
Spaces are always available.
Contact childcare@linst.ac.uk or 020 7514 6528 for further details.

General

There are societies or organised social activities for mature students.
Work experience is taken into consideration as well as academic
qualifications for mature students on application.

London College of Printing

Elephant and Castle
London
SE1 6SB
Phone: 020 7514 6569
Fax: 020 7514 8896
Email: info@lcp.linst.ac.uk
Website: www.lcp.linst.ac.uk

Student Support Officer

Celia Bishop
Phone: 020 7514 6607
Email: cbishop@lcp.linst.ac.uk

Applications

General entry qualifications that are considered acceptable for mature
applicants without the normal standard entry qualifications:

Access Course	Yes
APEL/APL	Yes

Funding

There are no specific mature student bursaries available over and above the
national funds.

Study

Negotiated flexible learning is available on most courses. It is available to:

Full-time students	Yes
Part-time students	Yes
Distance Learning students	Yes

Timetabling hours

Some modules can be studied that require attending only morning lectures.

Accommodation and childcare

Accommodation is available:

Specifically for mature students	No
For mature students with families	No

The institution does have crèche/childcare facilities.
There are 34 spaces.
Spaces are not always available.

General

Mature applicants are very welcome.

London School of Economics and Political Science

Houghton Street
London
WC2A 2AE
Phone: 020 7955 6613
Fax: 020 7955 7421
Email: stu.rec@lse.ac.uk
Website: www.lse.ac.uk
Total number of students at institution: 7,000

Mature Students' Officer

Phone: 020 7955 7158
Email: j.clark@lse.ac.uk

Applications

General entry qualifications that are considered acceptable for mature applicants without the normal standard entry qualifications:

Access Course	Yes
Essay submission	Yes
Entrance exam	Yes
Other	Open University degree

The institution does interview all mature applicants.

Study

Negotiated flexible learning is not available on most courses.

Timetabling hours

Lectures are timetabled between 9am and 6pm.

Accommodation and childcare

Accommodation is available:

Specifically for mature students	No
For mature students with families	No

The institution does have crèche/childcare facilities.

There are spaces for 9 babies and 16 children.

Spaces are not always available.

Help with the cost of this nursery is available for student parents in hardship.

The Students' Union runs a playgroup for school-aged children of students and staff during the half-term holidays.

General

There are societies or organised social activities for mature students. There is a mature students' society.

There is online information specifically for mature students at www.lse.ac.uk/collections/LSESU/.

Loughborough College
Radmoor Road
Loughborough
Leicestershire
LE11 3BT
Phone: 01509 618388
Website: www.loucoll.ac.uk

Student Support Officer
Alan Tsong
Phone: 01509 618295
Email: tsonga@loucoll.ac.uk

Applications
General entry qualifications that are considered acceptable for mature applicants without the normal standard entry qualifications:

Access Course	Yes
Essay submission	No
Entrance exam	No
APEL/APL	Yes

The institution does interview all mature applicants.

Funding
There are no specific mature student bursaries available over and above the national funds.

Study
Negotiated flexible learning is available on most courses.
It is available to:

Full-time students	No
Part-time students	Yes
Distance Learning students	Yes

Timetabling hours
Lectures are timetabled between 9am and 6pm.

Accommodation and childcare
Accommodation is available:

Specifically for mature students	No
For mature students with families	No

The institution does have crèche/childcare facilities.
Spaces are not always available.

General
There are no societies or organised social activities for mature students.

Loughborough University
Loughborough
Leicestershire
LE11 3TU
Phone: 01509 223522
Fax: 01509 223905
Email: admissions@lboro.ac.uk
Website: www.lboro.ac.uk
Total number of students at institution: 12,500
Total number of mature students: approximately 720 (undergraduate only)

Student Advice
Phone: 01509 632017
Email: lsu.advice@lboro.ac.uk

Applications
General entry qualifications that are considered acceptable for mature
applicants without the normal standard entry qualifications:

Access Course	Yes
Essay submission	No
Entrance exam	No
APEL/APL	Yes

The institution does not interview all mature applicants, but has an
agreement to interview local mature Access students.

Funding
There are specific mature student bursaries available over and above the
national funds.

Study

Negotiated flexible learning is not available on most courses.

Timetabling hours

Lectures are timetabled between 9am and 6pm.

Modules cannot be studied that require attending only morning lectures.

Accommodation and childcare

Accommodation is available:

Specifically for mature students	No
For mature students with families	Yes

The institution does have crèche/childcare facilities.

Spaces are not always available.

General

There are societies or organised social activities for mature students.

These are organised by the Mature Students' Association.

Lowestoft College

St Peters Street
Lowestoft
Suffolk
NR32 2NB
Phone: 01502 583521
Fax: 01502 500031
Email: info@lowestoft.ac.uk
Website: www.lowestoft.ac.uk
Total number of students at institution: 7,100
Total number of mature students: 5,400

Student Support Officer

Bridget Bannister
Phone: 01502 525060
Fax: 01502 500031
Email: b.banister@lowestoft.ac.uk

Applications

General entry qualifications that are considered acceptable for mature applicants without the normal standard entry qualifications:

Access Course	Yes
Essay submission	Yes
Entrance exam	No
APEL/APL	Yes

The institution does interview all mature applicants.

Funding

There are no specific mature student bursaries available over and above the national funds.

Study

Negotiated flexible learning is not available on most courses.
It is available to:

Full-time students	No
Part-time students	No
Distance Learning students	Yes

Timetabling hours

Lectures are timetabled between 9.00am and 4.30pm, and 6.00pm and 9.00pm.

Accommodation and childcare

Accommodation is available:

Specifically for mature students	No
For mature students with families	No

The institution does have crèche/childcare facilities.
Spaces are not always available.

General

There are no societies or organised social activities for mature students.

Lucy Cavendish College
Lady Margaret Road
Cambridge
CB3 0BU
Phone: 01223 330280
Fax: 01223 332178
Email: lcc-admissions@lists.cam.ac.uk
Website: www.lucy-cav.cam.ac.uk
Total number of students at institution: 224
Total number of mature students: 224

Student Support Officer
Phone: 01223 330280
Fax: 01223 332178
Email: lcc-admissions@lists.cam.ac.uk

Applications
General entry qualifications that are considered acceptable for mature applicants without the normal standard entry qualifications:

Access Course	Yes
Essay submission	No
Entrance exam	No
APEL/APL	No
Other	Open University courses; Certificate in HE.

The institution does not interview all mature applicants.

Funding
There are specific mature student bursaries available over and above the national funds.

Study
Negotiated flexible learning is not available on most courses.

Timetabling hours
Lecture times vary.
Modules can be studied that require attending only morning lectures.

Accommodation and childcare
Accommodation is available:

Specifically for mature students	Yes – all accommodation is for mature students.
For mature students with families	Yes – some family accommodation is available.

The institution does not have crèche/childcare facilities.
Childcare bursaries are available.

General
There are societies or organised social activities for mature students.
As a mature college, all activities are geared towards mature students.
There is online information specifically for mature students at www.lucy-cav.cam.ac.uk and at the main University of Cambridge website:
www.cam.ac.uk
Lucy Cavendish is for mature (21 years of age and above) women only and is one of four Cambridge colleges admitting only mature students.
Prospective applicants are encouraged to make contact with the admissions office as early as possible to obtain help and advice when applying.

University of Luton
Park Square
Luton
Bedfordshire
LU1 3JU
Phone: 01582 734111
Fax: 01582 743400
Email: enquiries@luton.ac.uk
Website: www.luton.ac.uk

Mature Students' Officer
Phone: 01582 489366
Fax: 01582 457187
Email: su.maturestudentofficer@luton.ac.uk

Student Support Officer
Mohamed Farooqi
Phone: 01582 743275
Fax: 01582 457187
Email: Mohamed.farooqi@luton.ac.uk

Applications
General entry qualifications that are considered acceptable for mature applicants without the normal standard entry qualifications:

Other	Experience in the workplace.

Accommodation and childcare
The institution does not have crèche/childcare facilities.
A childcare group is available during half-terms.

University of Manchester
Oxford Road
Manchester
M13 9PL
Phone: 0161 275 2000
Email: ug.admissions@man.ac.uk
Website: www.man.ac.uk
Total number of students at institution: 20,000
Total number of mature students: 4,000

Mature Students' Adviser
Phone: 0161 275 3298
Email: phil.eva@man.ac.uk

Applications
General entry qualifications that are considered acceptable for mature applicants without the normal standard entry qualifications:

Access Course	Yes
Essay submission	No
Entrance exam	No
APEL/APL	No

The institution normally interviews all mature applicants.

Funding

There are specific mature student bursaries available over and above the national funds. The university offers a 'Gateway' bursary of £2,000 to students from specified target groups, of which mature students comprise one. A high proportion of these awards go to mature students.

Study

Negotiated flexible learning is not available on most courses.

Timetabling hours

Lectures are timetabled between 9am and 5pm.
Modules can be studied that require attending only morning lectures.

Accommodation and childcare

Accommodation is available:

Specifically for mature students	Yes – one large hall is reserved for mature undergraduates and postgraduates.
For mature students with families	Yes – several small halls cater for married couples and families.

The institution does have crèche/childcare facilities.
There are 50 spaces.
Spaces are not always available.
Extensive information on childcare in Manchester is available from the Mature Students' Adviser.

General

The Burlington Society for mature undergraduates and postgraduates organises social activities for mature students.
There is online information specifically for mature students at www.man.ac.uk/study/mature and www.burlington.man.ac.uk/index.html

University of Manchester Institute of Science and Technology (UMIST)

PO Box 88
Manchester
M60 1QD
Phone: 0161 236 3311
Fax: 0161 200 4019
Website: www.umist.ac.uk
Total number of students at institution: 6,747

Mature Students' Officer

Phone: 0161 236 3311
Email: j.roocroft@student.umist.ac.uk

Student Support Officer

Phone: 0161 200 5757
Email: studentsupport@umist.ac.uk

Applications

General entry qualifications that are considered acceptable for mature applicants without the normal standard entry qualifications:

Access Course	Yes
Other	Life and work experience.

The institution does not interview all mature applicants.

Funding

There are no specific mature student bursaries available over and above the national funds.

Accommodation and childcare

Accommodation is available:

Specifically for mature students	No
For mature students with families	Yes – rooms and flats.

The institution does have crèche/childcare facilities.
There are 48 spaces.
Spaces are not always available.

General

The Burlington Society is for mature and postgraduate students.
There is online information specifically for mature students, such as entry requirements, accommodation etc.

Mid-Cheshire College

Hartford Campus
Chester Road
Northwich
Cheshire
CW8 1LJ
Phone: 01606 74444
Fax: 01606 720700
Email: info@midchesh.ac.uk
Website: www.midchesh.ac.uk
Total number of students at institution: 1,800 full-time, 6,000 part-time
Total number of mature students: 6,000

Student Support Officer

Joan Mills
Phone: 01606 74444
Fax: 01606 720700
Email: jmills@midchesh.ac.uk

Applications

General entry qualifications that are considered acceptable for mature applicants without the normal standard entry qualifications:

Other	Individual interview.

The institution interviews mature applicants for full-time courses only.

Study

Negotiated flexible learning is available to:

Full-time students	Yes
Part-time students	Yes
Distance Learning students	Yes

Timetabling hours

Modules can be studied that require attending only morning lectures.

Accommodation and childcare

Accommodation is available:

Specifically for mature students	No – this is a non-residential FE college.
For mature students with families	No – this is a non-residential FE college.

The institution does have crèche/childcare facilities.
Spaces are always available.

General

There are no societies or organised social activities for mature students.
Mid-Cheshire College prides itself on its friendly and supportive
atmosphere.

Moray College

Moray Street
Elgin
Scotland
IV30 1JJ
Phone: 01343 576000
Fax: 01343 576001
Email: mc.registry@moray.uhi.ac.uk
Website: www.moray.ac.uk
Total number of students at institution: 7,000
Total number of mature students: 4,850

Student Support Officer

Heather Henderson
Phone: 01343 576269
Fax: 01343 576001
Email: heather.henderson@moray.uhi.ac.uk

Applications

General entry qualifications that are considered acceptable for mature applicants without the normal standard entry qualifications:

Access Course	Yes
APEL/APL	Yes
Other	Interview

The institution does not automatically interview all mature applicants.

Funding

There are no specific mature student bursaries available over and above the national funds.

Study

Negotiated flexible learning is available on most courses.
It is available to:

Full-time students	No
Part-time students	Yes
Distance Learning students	Yes

Timetabling hours

Lectures are generally timetabled between 9.00am and 4.00pm.
Modules can be studied that require attending only morning lectures.

Accommodation and childcare

Accommodation is available:

Specifically for mature students	No
For mature students with families	No

The institution does have crèche/childcare facilities.
There are 60 spaces.
Spaces are not always available.

General

There are no societies or organised social activities specifically for mature students.

Neath Port Talbot College

Dwy-r-Felin Road
Neath
SA10 7RF
Phone: 01639 648000
Fax: 01639 648009
Email: admissions@nptc.ac.uk
Website: www.nptc.ac.uk
Total number of full-time and part-time students at institution: 14,000
Total number of adult students: 10,000
Total number of full-time mature students: 150

Mature Students' Officer

Phone: 01639 648000
Fax: 01639 648009
Email: admissions@nptc.ac.uk

Student Support Officer

Lynda Dix
Phone: 01639 648404
Fax: 01639 648009
Email: lynda.dix@nptc.ac.uk

Applications

General entry qualifications that are considered acceptable for mature
applicants without the normal standard entry qualifications:

Access Course	Yes
Other	Interview

The institution does interview all mature applicants.

Funding

There are no specific mature student bursaries available over and above the
national funds.

Study

Negotiated flexible learning is available on most courses.
It is available to:

Full-time students	Yes
Part-time students	Yes
Distance Learning students	No

Timetabling hours
Lectures are timetabled between 9am to 9pm.
Modules can be studied that require attending only morning lectures.

Accommodation and childcare
Accommodation is available:

Specifically for mature students	No
For mature students with families	No

The institution does have crèche/childcare facilities.
There are 50 spaces.
Spaces are usually available.

General
There are no societies or organised social activities for mature students.
Neath Port Talbot College is a further education college with a small
number of HE courses. Most adults attending the college are on non-
advanced courses.

Newcastle College
Rye Hill Campus
Scotswood Road
Newcastle upon Tyne
NE4 5BR
Phone: 0191 200 4000
Fax: 0191 200 4517
Email: enquiries@ncl-coll.ac.uk
Website: www.ncl-coll.ac.uk
Total number of students at institution: 36,453
Total number of mature students: 25,000

Applications
General entry qualifications that are considered acceptable for mature
applicants without the normal standard entry qualifications:

Access Course	Yes
Other	Previous experience/ qualifications.

Funding

There are no specific mature student bursaries available over and above the national funds.

Study

Negotiated flexible learning is not available on most courses.
It is available to:

Full-time students	No
Part-time students	Yes
Distance Learning students	Yes

Timetabling hours

Lectures are timetabled between 9.00am and 9.00pm.
Some modules can be studied that require attending only morning lectures.

Accommodation and childcare

Accommodation is available:

Specifically for mature students	No
For mature students with families	No

The institution does have crèche/childcare facilities.
There are 25 spaces.
Spaces are not always available.

General

There are no societies or organised social activities for mature students.
Mature students are welcome to apply for any course – the college operates an equal opportunities policy.

Newcastle-under-Lyme College

Liverpool Road
Newcastle-under-Lyme
Staffordshire
ST5 2DF
Phone: 01782 715111
Fax: 01782 717396
Email: enquiries@nulc.ac.uk
Website: www.nulc.ac.uk
Total number of students at institution: over 10,000
Total number of mature students: over 8,000

Student Support Officer

Gary Hurlstone
Phone: 01782 254391
Fax: 01782 717396

Applications

General entry qualifications that are considered acceptable for mature
applicants without the normal standard entry qualifications:

Access Course	Yes
Essay submission	No
Entrance exam	No
APEL/APL	Yes

The institution does not interview all mature applicants.

Funding

There are no specific mature student bursaries available over and above the
national funds.

Study

Negotiated flexible learning is available on some courses.
It is available to:

Full-time students	Yes – some
Part-time students	Yes – some
Distance Learning students	Yes – some

Timetabling hours

Lectures are timetabled between 8.30am and 9.30pm Monday to Friday; 9am and 1pm Saturday.

Modules can be studied that require attending only morning lectures.

Accommodation and childcare

Accommodation is available:

Specifically for mature students	No
For mature students with families	No

The institution does not have crèche/childcare facilities.

General

There are no societies or organised social activities for mature students.

University of Newcastle upon Tyne

6 Kensington Terrace
Newcastle upon Tyne
NE1 7RU
Phone: 0191 222 5527
Fax: 0191 222 8685
Email: mature-students-enquiries@ncl.ac.uk
Website: www.ncl.ac.uk
Total number of students at institution: 16,339
Total number of mature students: 2,700

Mature Students' Officer

c/o Union Society
Phone: 0191 222 1876
Email: union.society@ncl.ac.uk

Student Support Officer

Phone: 0191 222 5525
Email: mature-student-support@ncl.ac.uk

Applications

General entry qualifications that are considered acceptable for mature applicants without the normal standard entry qualifications:

Access Course	Yes
Essay submission	No
Entrance exam	No
APEL/APL	No

The institution does not interview all mature applicants.

Funding
There are specific mature student bursaries available over and above the national funds.

Study
Negotiated flexible learning is not available on most courses.

Timetabling hours
Lectures are timetabled between 9am and 6pm.
Modules cannot be studied that require attending only morning lectures.

Accommodation and childcare
Accommodation is available:

Specifically for mature students	Yes
For mature students with families	Yes

The institution does not have crèche/childcare facilities.
Childcare support officer 0191 222 3599; childcare@ncl.ac.uk

General
There are societies or organised social activities for mature students. There is a Postgraduate and Mature Students' Society.
There is online information specifically for mature students at www.ncl.ac.uk/undergraduate/further/mature/.

Newman College of Higher Education
Genners Lane
Bartley Green
Birmingham
B32 2NT
Phone: 0121 476 1181

Email: registry@newman.ac.uk
Website: www.newman.ac.uk
Total number of students at institution: 1,691
Total number of mature students: 583

Student Support Officer
Robin Gutteridge
Email: r.m.gutteridge@newman.ac.uk

Applications
General entry qualifications that are considered acceptable for mature applicants without the normal standard entry qualifications:

Access Course	Yes
Essay submission	No
Entrance exam	No
APEL/APL	Yes

The institution does not interview all mature applicants.

Funding
There are no specific mature student bursaries available over and above the national funds.

Study
Negotiated flexible learning is not available on most courses.

Timetabling hours
Lectures are timetabled between 9.15am and 5.45pm.
Modules cannot be studied that require attending only morning lectures.

Accommodation and childcare
Accommodation is available:

Specifically for mature students	No
For mature students with families	No

The institution does not have crèche/childcare facilities.

General
There are societies or organised social activities for mature students.
Newman has a history of successfully supporting mature students. The

small size of classes and interactive teaching style at Newman are often commended by mature students here.

North East Lincolnshire College of Higher Education

Nuns Corner
Grimsby
DN34 5BQ
Phone: 0800 328 3631
Fax: 01472 315506
Email: headmissions@grimsby.ac.uk
Website: www.grimsby.ac.uk

Student Support Officer

Diane Payne
Phone: 01472 311222 ext. 226
Fax: 01472 315506
Email: payned@grimsby.ac.uk

Applications

General entry qualifications that are considered acceptable for mature applicants without the normal standard entry qualifications:

Access Course	Yes
Essay submission	No
Entrance exam	No
APEL/APL	Yes

The institution does not interview all mature applicants.

Funding

There are no specific mature student bursaries available over and above the national funds.

Study

Negotiated flexible learning is available on most courses.
It is available to:

Full-time students	No
Part-time students	Yes

Timetabling hours

Lectures are timetabled between 10am and 3pm if possible.

Modules can be studied that require attending only morning lectures.

Accommodation and childcare

Accommodation is available:

Specifically for mature students	No
For mature students with families	No

The institution does have crèche/childcare facilities.

Spaces are always available.

Contact the Children's Centre on 01472 311222 ext. 530

General

There are no societies or organised social activities for mature students, but the institution is working to improve this.

North Tyneside College

Embleton Avenue
Wallsend
Tyne and Wear
NE28 9NJ
Phone: 0191 229 5000
Fax: 0191 229 5301
Email: steve.telford@ntyneside.ac.uk
Website: www.ntyneside.ac.uk
Total number of students at institution: 15,000
Total number of mature students: 12,000

Applications

General entry qualifications that are considered acceptable for mature applicants without the normal standard entry qualifications:

Access Course	Yes
APEL/APL	Yes

The institution does not interview all mature applicants.

Funding
There are no specific mature student bursaries available over and above the national funds.

Study
Negotiated flexible learning is available on most courses.
It is available to:

Full-time students	Yes
Part-time students	Yes
Distance Learning students	Yes

Timetabling hours
Lectures are timetabled between 9am and 9pm.
Modules can be studied that require attending only morning lectures.

Accommodation and childcare
Accommodation is available:

Specifically for mature students	No
For mature students with families	No

The institution does have crèche/childcare facilities.
There are 37 spaces.
Spaces are not always available.

General
There are no societies or organised social activities for mature students.

Northbrook College, Sussex
Littlehampton Road
Worthing
West Sussex
BN12 6NU
Phone: 01903 606060
Fax: 01903 606073
Email: enquiries@nbcol.ac.uk
Website: www.northbrook.ac.uk

Total number of students at institution: under 20,000
Total number of mature students: 16,000 (80 per cent)

Advice and Admissions Manager

Brenda Cook
Phone: 01903 606005
Fax: 01903 606073
Email: enquiries@nbcol.ac.uk

Applications

General entry qualifications that are considered acceptable for mature applicants without the normal standard entry qualifications:

Access Course	Yes
Essay submission	Yes
Entrance exam	No
APEL/APL	Yes
Other	Portfolio submission, audition etc.

The institution does not interview all mature applicants.

Funding

There are no specific mature student bursaries available over and above the national funds.

Study

Negotiated flexible learning is available on most courses.
It is available to:

Full-time students	Yes
Part-time students	Yes
Distance Learning students	No

Timetabling hours

Lectures are timetabled between 9am and 9pm.
Modules can be studied that require attending only morning lectures.

Accommodation and childcare

Accommodation is available:

Specifically for mature students	No
For mature students with families	No

The institution does have crèche/childcare facilities.
There are 20 spaces.
Spaces are not always available.

General

There are no societies or organised social activities for mature students.
There is online information specifically for mature students.

Northern College

Wentworth Castle
Stainborough
Barnsley
S75 3ET
Phone: 01226 776000
Fax: 01226 776025
Email: studentservices@northern.ac.uk
Website: www.northern.ac.uk
Total number of students at institution: 4,500
Total number of mature students: 4,500

Student Support Officer

Beth Hutchinson
Phone: 01226 776000 ext. 6075
Fax: 01226 776025
Email: b.hutchinson@northern.ac.uk

Applications

General entry qualifications that are considered acceptable for mature
applicants without the normal standard entry qualifications:

Other	Each student is considered on his or her own merits.

The institution does interview mature applicants for some courses.

Funding
There are specific mature student bursaries available over and above the national funds.

Study
Negotiated flexible learning is available on most courses.
It is available to:

Full-time students	Yes
Part-time students	Yes

Timetabling hours
Modules can be studied that require attending only morning lectures.

Accommodation and childcare
Accommodation is available:

Specifically for mature students	Yes
For mature students with families	Yes

The institution does have crèche/childcare facilities.
Spaces are always available.
Childcare is free at Northern College.

General
There are societies or organised social activities for mature students.

Northern School of Contemporary Dance
98 Chapeltown Road
Leeds
LS7 4BH
Phone: 0113 219 3019
Fax: 0113 219 3030
Website: www.nscd.ac.uk
Total number of students at institution: 202
Total number of mature students: 80

Applications
General entry qualifications that are considered acceptable for mature applicants without the normal standard entry qualifications:

Access Course	Yes
Essay submission	Yes
APEL/APL	Yes

The institution does interview all mature applicants.

Funding

There are no specific mature student bursaries available over and above the national funds.

Study

Negotiated flexible learning is not available on most courses.

Timetabling hours

Lectures are timetabled between 8.45am and 6.00pm.

Modules cannot be studied that require attending only morning lectures.

Accommodation and childcare

Accommodation is available:

Specifically for mature students	No
For mature students with families	No

The institution does not have crèche/childcare facilities.

General

There are no societies or organised social activities for mature students.

Norton Radstock College

South Hill Park

Radstock

BA3 3RW

Phone: 01761 433161

Fax: 01761 436173

Email: courses@nortcoll.ac.uk

Website: www.nortcoll.ac.uk

Total number of students at institution: 5,500

Total number of mature students: 4,664

Mature Students' Officer

Phone: 01761 433161 ext. 429
Email: jnoel@nortcoll.ac.uk

Applications

General entry qualifications that are considered acceptable for mature
applicants without the normal standard entry qualifications:

Access Course	Yes
Other	Interview

The institution does interview all mature applicants.

Funding

There are specific mature student bursaries available over and above the
national funds.

Study

Negotiated flexible learning is available on most courses.
It is available to:

Full-time students	Yes
Part-time students	Yes

Timetabling hours

Lectures are timetabled between 9am and 9.30pm.
Modules can be studied that require attending only morning lectures.

Accommodation and childcare

Accommodation is available:

Specifically for mature students	No
For mature students with families	No

The institution does have crèche/childcare facilities.
There are 48 spaces.
Spaces are not always available.

General

There are no societies or organised social activities for mature students.

University of Nottingham

University Park
Nottingham
NG7 2RD
Phone: 0115 951 5151
Fax: 0115 951 3666
Website: www.nottingham.ac.uk
Total number of students at institution: 28,000
Total number of mature students: 1,960

Head of Student Support

Robin Dollery
Phone: 0115 951 5767
Email: robin.dollery@nottingham.ac.uk

Applications

General entry qualifications that are considered acceptable for mature
applicants without the normal standard entry qualifications:

Access Course	Yes
Essay submission	No
Entrance exam	No
APEL/APL	Yes – taken into consideration with other factors, depending on the faculty.

The institution does not interview all mature applicants.

Funding

There are no specific mature student bursaries available over and above the
national funds.

Study

Negotiated flexible learning is not available on most courses.
Some faculties offer degrees on a part-time study basis.

Timetabling hours

Lectures are timetabled between 9am and 6pm.
Modules can be studied that require attending only morning lectures.

Accommodation and childcare

Accommodation is available:

Specifically for mature students	Yes – but not guaranteed.
For mature students with families	Yes – but not guaranteed.

The institution does have crèche/childcare facilities.
Spaces are not always available.
Student Support can give information on childcare.

General

The Mature Students' Guild organises social activities for mature students.
There is online information specifically for mature students at
http://www.nottingham.ac.uk/prospectuses/undergrad/introduction/applying/
mature.phtml.
The School of Continuing Education offers the Open Studies programme,
which requires no formal qualifications and can build up to a BA in
combined studies.

Nottingham Trent University

Burton Street
Nottingham
NG1 4BU
Phone: 0115 941 8418
Fax: 0115 848 6503
Email: cor.web@ntu.ac.uk
Website: www.ntu.ac.uk
Total number of students at institution: 23,094
Total number of mature students: 4,619 (i.e. 20 per cent)

Mature Students' Officer

Kathryn Frith
Phone: 0115 848 3290
Fax: 0115 848 6665
Email: kathryn.frith@ntu.ac.uk

Student Support Officer
Sally Olohan
Phone: 0115 848 2971
Email: sally.olohan@ntu.ac.uk

Applications
Contact the admissions tutor for specific information regarding general entry qualifications that are considered acceptable for mature applicants without the normal standard entry qualifications.

The institution does not interview all mature applicants.

Funding
There are specific mature student bursaries available over and above the national funds.

Study
Negotiated flexible learning may be available on some courses depending on the programme of study.

Accommodation and childcare
Accommodation is available:

Specifically for mature students	No
For mature students with families	No

The institution does not have crèche/childcare facilities.

General
There are societies or organised social activities for mature students, organised by the student support service.

There is online information specifically for mature students at www.ntu.ac.uk/sss/mature.

A pre-entry guide for prospective mature students (2004 entry) is available from Student Support Services.

Oldham College
Rochdale Road
Oldham
OL9 6AA
Phone: 0161 624 5214

Fax: 0161 785 4234
Email: info@oldham.ac.uk
Website: www.oldham.ac.uk
Total number of students at institution: 10,000
Total number of mature students: 7,000

Mature Students' Officer

Phone: 0161 785 4054
Fax: 0161 785 4234
Email: alan.bickerstaffe@oldham.ac.uk

Student Support Officer

Phone: 0161 785 4054
Fax: 0161 785 4234
Email: patricia.walkington@oldham.ac.uk

Applications

General entry qualifications that are considered acceptable for mature applicants without the normal standard entry qualifications:

Access Course	Yes
Essay submission	No
Entrance exam	No
APL	Yes

The institution does interview all mature applicants.

Funding

There are no specific mature student bursaries available over and above the national funds.

Study

Negotiated flexible learning is not available on most courses.

Timetabling hours

Lectures are timetabled between 9am and 9pm.
Modules can be studied that require attending only morning lectures.

Accommodation and childcare

Accommodation is available:

Specifically for mature students	No
For mature students with families	No

The institution does have crèche/childcare facilities.
There are 50 spaces.
Spaces are not always available.
The institution provides financial help for childcare to the most needy students.

General
There are no specific societies or organised social activities for mature students, only the general students' union social activities.
There is no online information specifically for mature students.

Open University
Watton Hall
Milton Keynes
MK7 6AA
Phone: 01908 653231
Fax: 01908 652247
Email: ces-gen@open.ac.uk
Website: www.open.ac.uk
Total number of students at institution: 180,000

Study
Negotiated flexible learning is available on most courses.
It is available to Distance Learning students.

Accommodation and childcare
Accommodation and childcare are not available.
The Open University is a distance learning not campus-based institution.
The Open University has an open access policy and therefore attracts many mature students who do not have the academic qualifications to study at conventional universities. About a third of the OU's graduates gain their degrees without having the A-levels that are normally essential for entry into other institutions. The university's open access policy includes the ongoing work by the Centre for Widening Participation, which initiates projects and partnerships to ensure as wide a cross-section of the population as possible has access to higher education.

Oxford Brookes University
Gipsy Lane
Headington
Oxford
OX3 0BP
Phone: 01865 483040
Fax: 01865 483983
Email: admissions@brookes.ac.uk
Website: www.brookes.ac.uk

Mature Students' Adviser
Phone: 01865 484657

Applications
General entry qualifications that are considered acceptable for mature
applicants without the normal standard entry qualifications:

Access Course	Yes
Essay submission	No
Entrance exam	No
APEL/APL	Yes

The institution does not interview all mature applicants.

Funding
There are no specific mature student bursaries available over and above the
national funds.

Study
Negotiated flexible learning is not available on most courses.
It is available to:

Full-time students	No
Part-time students	No
Distance Learning students	Yes

Timetabling hours
Lectures are timetabled between 9.00am and 6.00pm.
Some modules can be studied that require attending only morning lectures.

Accommodation and childcare

Accommodation is available:

Specifically for mature students	No
For mature students with families	No

The institution does have crèche/childcare facilities.
Spaces are not always available.

University of Paisley

Paisley
PA1 2BE
Phone: 0800 027 1000
Fax: 0141 848 3333
Email: uni-direct@paisley.ac.uk
Website: www.paisley.ac.uk
Total number of students at institution: 10,500
Total number of mature students: 3150–4200 (approx. 30–40 per cent)

Student Advisory Service

Phone: 0141 848 3803
Fax: 0141 848 3804
Email: careers@wpmail.paisley.ac.uk

Applications

General entry qualifications that are considered acceptable for mature
applicants without the normal standard entry qualifications:

Access Course	Yes
Essay submission	No
Entrance exam	No
APEL/APL	Yes
Other	Each case is assessed individually.

The institution does not automatically interview all mature applicants, but
it depends on individual circumstances.

Funding
There are specific mature student bursaries available over and above the national funds.

Study
Negotiated flexible learning is available on most courses.
It is available to:

Full-time students	No
Part-time students	Yes
Distance Learning students	Yes

Timetabling hours
Lectures are timetabled between 9am and 5.30pm for full-time students, between 6pm and 9pm for part-time evening students and between 9am and 12pm for part-time weekend students.

Accommodation and childcare
Accommodation is available:

Specifically for mature students	No
For mature students with families	No

The institution does have crèche/childcare facilities.
Spaces are not always available as the nursery is at full capacity and has a waiting list.

General
There are no societies or organised social activities for mature students.

People's College
Maid Marian Way
Nottingham
NG1 6AB
Phone: 0115 912 3444
Fax: 0115 912 8600
Email: admissions@peoples.ac.uk
Website: www.peoples.ac.uk
Total number of students at institution: 12,000
Total number of mature students: 10,000

Student Support Officer
Vicky Harsant
Phone: 0115 912 8622
Fax: 0115 912 8600
Email: vicky.harsant@peoples.ac.uk

Applications
General entry qualifications that are considered acceptable for mature
applicants without the normal standard entry qualifications:

Access Course	No
Essay submission	No
Entrance exam	No
APEL/APL	No

The institution does not interview all mature applicants.

Funding
There are no specific mature student bursaries available over and above the
national funds.

Study
Negotiated flexible learning is available on some courses.
It is available to:

Full-time students	No
Part-time students	No
Distance Learning students	Yes

Timetabling hours
Lectures are timetabled between 9am and 9pm.
Modules cannot be studied that require attending only morning lectures.

Accommodation and childcare
Accommodation is available:

Specifically for mature students	No
For mature students with families	No

The institution does have crèche/childcare facilities.
There are 67 spaces in total at two centres.
Spaces are not always available.

General
There are no societies or organised social activities for mature students.
There is online information specifically for mature students: select 'Adult
Learning' from the homepage.

University of Portsmouth
University House
Winston Churchill Avenue
Portsmouth
PO1 2UP
Phone: 023 9284 8484
Fax: 023 9284 3082
Email: admissions@port.ac.uk
Website: www.port.ac.uk
Total number of students at institution: 24,552
Total number of mature students: 14,290

Student Advice Services
Phone: 023 9284 3157
Fax: 023 9284 3430
Email: adviceatnuffield@port.ac.uk

Applications
General entry qualifications that are considered acceptable for mature
applicants without the normal standard entry qualifications:

Access Course	Yes
Essay submission	No
Entrance exam	No
APEL/APL	Yes

The institution does not interview all mature applicants.

Funding
There are specific mature student bursaries available over and above the
national funds.

Study
Negotiated flexible learning is not available on most courses.

Timetabling hours

Lectures are timetabled between 8am and 6pm.

Modules cannot be studied that require attending only morning lectures.

Accommodation and childcare

Accommodation is available:

Specifically for mature students	No
For mature students with families	No

The institution does have crèche/childcare facilities.

There are 38 spaces.

Spaces are not always available.

There is a university nursery.

General

Contact the students' union on 023 9284 3640 for advice on societies or organised social activities for mature students.

There is online information specifically for mature students: some departmental details and finance information.

Queen Margaret University College

Corstorphine Campus

Clerwood Terrace

Edinburgh

EH12 8TS

Phone: 0131 317 3000

Fax: 0131 317 3248

Email: admissions@qmuc.ac.uk

Website: www.qmuc.ac.uk

Transition and Pre-entry Guidance Adviser

Jenni Murray

Phone: 0131 317 3376

Fax: 0131 317 3185

Email: jmurray@qmuc.ac.uk

Applications

General entry qualifications that are considered acceptable for mature applicants without the normal standard entry qualifications:

Access Course	Yes
Essay submission	Yes – occasionally, for some courses.
Entrance exam	No
APEL/APL	No
Other	Foundation courses.

The institution does not interview all mature applicants.

Funding

There are no specific mature student bursaries available over and above the national funds.

Study

Negotiated flexible learning is available on some courses.
It is available to:

Full-time students	No
Part-time students	Yes
Distance Learning students	Yes

Timetabling hours

Lectures are timetabled between 9.15am and 7.15pm (9.15am and 8.15pm on Tuesdays and Thursdays).
Modules can be studied that require attending only morning lectures.

Accommodation and childcare

Accommodation is available:

Specifically for mature students	Yes – but for international students only.
For mature students with families	No – but accommodation lists can be provided.

The institution does not have crèche/childcare facilities.
The Pre-entry Guidance Adviser can offer advice about childcare provision.

General

Social activities for mature students are occasionally organised by the Mature Students' Officer.

Prospective mature students can contact the Pre-entry Guidance Adviser at any stage to discuss their plans.

Queen Mary, University of London

Mile End Road
London
E1 4NS
Phone: 0800 376 1800
Fax: 020 7882 3703
Email: admissions@qmul.ac.uk
Website: www.qmul.ac.uk
Total number of students at institution: 9,600
Total number of mature students: 1,355

Advice Service

Phone: 020 7882 5175
Email: welfare@qmul.ac.uk

Applications

General entry qualifications that are considered acceptable for mature applicants without the normal standard entry qualifications:

Access Course	Yes
Essay submission	No
Entrance exam	Yes
APEL/APL	Yes

The institution does interview all mature applicants.

Funding

There are no specific mature student bursaries available over and above the national funds.

Study

Negotiated flexible learning is not available on most courses.

Timetabling hours

Lectures are timetabled between 9am and 5pm.

Modules can be studied that require attending only morning lectures.

Accommodation and childcare

Accommodation is available:

Specifically for mature students	Yes – accommodation is set aside for mature students, subject to number of applications and availability.
For mature students with families	Yes – limited to four flats.

The institution does have crèche/childcare facilities.

Spaces are not always available.

Students may be eligible for assistance with fees.

General

There are societies or organised social activities for mature students.

Contact the students' union on 020 7882 5390 for details.

Queen's University Belfast

University Road

Belfast

BT7 1NN

Phone: 028 9033 5081

Fax: 028 9024 7895

Email: admissions@qub.ac.uk

Website: www.qub.ac.uk

Total number of students at institution: 16,000

Total number of mature students: 4,000

Mature Students' Officer

Phone: 028 9027 3106/08

Fax: 028 9023 6900

Email: su.mso@qub.ac.uk

Applications

General entry qualifications that are considered acceptable for mature applicants without the normal standard entry qualifications:

Access Course	Yes
Essay submission	No
Entrance exam	No
APEL/APL	No

The institution does not interview all mature applicants.

Funding

There are no specific mature student bursaries available over and above the national funds.

Study

Negotiated flexible learning is not available on most courses.

Timetabling hours

Lectures are timetabled between 9am and 6pm.
Some modules can be studied that require attending only morning lectures.

Accommodation and childcare

Accommodation is available:

Specifically for mature students	Yes – predominantly for postgraduate students.
For mature students with families	No

The institution does have crèche/childcare facilities.
There are 158 spaces, including 30 after-school spaces.
Spaces are not always available.
There is a summer scheme for over 200 children provided at Queen's Physical Education Centre.

General

There are societies or organised social activities for mature students. There is a Mature Students' Society within the Students' Union.
There is online information specifically for mature students at www.qubsu.org.

The Institute of Lifelong Learning at Queen's provides part-time study for both award- and non-award-bearing courses – attended mainly by mature students. Support is available on a course basis.

University of Reading
Whiteknights
PO Box 217
Reading
RG6 6AH
Phone: 0118 987 5123
Fax: 0118 931 4404
Email: information@reading.ac.uk
Website: www.reading.ac.uk
Total number of students at institution: c. 13,000
Total number of mature students: c. 1,590

Student Support Officer

Laura Kishore
Phone: 0118 378 6689
Fax: 0118 987 4722
Email: L.J.Kishore@reading.ac.uk

Applications
General entry qualifications that are considered acceptable for mature applicants without the normal standard entry qualifications:

Access Course	Yes
Essay submission	Yes – sometimes
	Entrance exam Yes
	– sometimes
APEL/APL	Yes – sometimes

The institution does not interview all mature applicants.

Funding
There are no specific mature student bursaries available over and above the national funds.

Study

Negotiated flexible learning is not available on most courses.

Timetabling hours

Lectures are timetabled between 9am and 6pm.

Modules can be studied that require attending only morning lectures.

Accommodation and childcare

Accommodation is available:

Specifically for mature students	Yes – there are flats reserved for mature students.
For mature students with families	Yes – there are flats reserved for students with families.

The institution does have crèche/childcare facilities.

There are 40 spaces.

There is also a campus pre-school as well as a full-time nursery.

General

There are societies or organised social activities for mature students.

There is online information specifically for mature students – www.reading.ac.uk/newstudents/mature.htm.

Rotherham College of Arts and Technology

Eastwood Lane

Rotherham

South Yorkshire

S65 1EG

Phone: 01709 362111

Fax: 01709 373053

Email: info@rotherham.ac.uk

Website: www.rotherham.ac.uk

Student Support Officer

Phone: 08080 722777

Applications

General entry qualifications that are considered acceptable for mature applicants without the normal standard entry qualifications:

Access Course	Yes
Essay submission	No
Entrance exam	No
APEL/APL	Yes
Other	Interview and review of skills in reading and using numbers.

The institution does interview all mature applicants.

Funding

There are no specific mature student bursaries available over and above the national funds.

Study

Negotiated flexible learning is not available on most courses.
It is available to:

Full-time students	No
Part-time students	Yes
Distance Learning students	Yes

Timetabling hours

Lectures are timetabled between 9.00am and 8.00pm.
Modules can be studied that require attending only morning lectures.

Accommodation and childcare

Accommodation is available:

Specifically for mature students	No
For mature students with families	No

The institution does have crèche/childcare facilities.
There are 80 spaces.
Spaces are always available.

We pay for external childcare if we have no places (for eligible students only).

General

There are no societies or organised social activities for mature students.

Royal Agricultural College

Cirencester
Gloucestershire
GL7 6JS
Phone: 01285 652531
Fax: 01285 641282
Email: admissions@rac.ac.uk
Website: www.rac.ac.uk
Total number of students at institution: 650
Total number of mature students: 195

Student Support Officer

Ron Coaten/Jane Brookes
Phone: 01285 652531
Fax: 01285 650219
Email: janebrookes@rac.ac.uk

Applications

General entry qualifications that are considered acceptable for mature applicants without the normal standard entry qualifications:

Access Course	Yes
APEL/APL	Yes

The institution does interview all mature applicants.

Funding

There are no specific mature student bursaries available over and above the national funds.

Study

Negotiated flexible learning is available on some courses.
It is available to:

Full-time students	No
Part-time students	Yes
Distance Learning students	No

Timetabling hours

Lectures are timetabled between 9.00am and 5.00pm.
Modules can be studied that require attending only morning lectures.

Accommodation and childcare

Accommodation is available:

Specifically for mature students	No
For mature students with families	No

The institution does not have crèche/childcare facilities.

General

There are societies or organised social activities for mature students. There is a mature students club.

Royal Scottish Academy of Music and Drama

100 Renfrew Street
Glasgow
G2 3DB
Phone: 0141 332 4101
Fax: 0141 332 8901
Email: s.daly@rsamd.ac.uk
Website: www.rsamd.ac.uk

Student Support Officer

Margaret Friday
Phone: 0141 270 8296
Email: supresident@rsamd.ac.uk

Applications

General entry qualifications that are considered acceptable for mature applicants without the normal standard entry qualifications:

Entrance exam	Yes

The institution does interview all mature applicants.

Funding
There are specific mature student bursaries available over and above the national funds.

Study
Negotiated flexible learning is only available to part-time students.

Timetabling hours
Modules cannot be studied that require attending only morning lectures.

Accommodation and childcare
Accommodation is available:

Specifically for mature students	No
For mature students with families	Yes

The institution does not have crèche/childcare facilities.

General
There are no societies or organised social activities for mature students.

Royal Welsh College of Music and Drama
Castle Grounds
Cathays Park
Cardiff
CF10 3ER
Phone: 029 2034 2854
Fax: 029 2039 1304
Email: info@rwcmd.ac.uk
Website: www.rwcmd.ac.uk
Total number of students at institution: 575
Total number of mature students: 139

Student Support Officer
Brian Weir
Phone: 029 2034 2854

Fax: 029 2039 1304
Email: weirba@rwcmd.ac.uk

Applications

General entry qualifications that are considered acceptable for mature
applicants without the normal standard entry qualifications:

Access Course	Yes
Essay submission	Yes
Entrance exam	No
APEL/APL	Yes

The institution does interview all mature applicants.

Funding

There are no specific mature student bursaries available over and above the
national funds.

Study

Negotiated flexible learning is not available on most courses.

Timetabling hours

Lectures are timetabled between 9.00am and 5.00pm.
Modules cannot be studied that require attending only morning lectures.

Accommodation and childcare

Accommodation is available:

Specifically for mature students	No
For mature students with families	No

The institution does not have crèche/childcare facilities.

General

There are no societies or organised social activities for mature students.
All applications are considered individually.

University of St Andrews

College Gate
North Street
St Andrews

Fife
KY16 9AJ
Phone: 01334 462150
Fax: 01334 462288
Email: admissions@st-and.ac.uk
Website: www.st-andrews.ac.uk
Total number of students at institution: 5,600
Total number of mature students: 500

Mature Students' Officer
Phone: 01334 462346
Fax: 01334 462208
Email: access@st-andrews.ac.uk

Applications
General entry qualifications that are considered acceptable for mature
applicants without the normal standard entry qualifications:

Access Course	Yes
Essay submission	No
Entrance exam	No
APEL/APL	Yes

The institution does not interview all mature applicants.

Funding
There are specific mature student bursaries available over and above the
national funds.

Study
Negotiated flexible learning is not available on most courses.

Timetabling hours
Lectures are timetabled between 9am and 5pm.
Modules can be studied that require attending only morning lectures.

Accommodation and childcare
Accommodation is available:

Specifically for mature students	Yes – by arrangement with the accommodation office.
For mature students with families	Yes – by arrangement with the accommodation office.

The institution does have crèche/childcare facilities.
Spaces are not always available.

General

There are societies or organised social activities for mature students.
A leaflet for mature students is available from the Access Centre.

St George's Hospital Medical School

Cranmer Terrace
London
SW17 0RE
Phone: 020 8725 5201
Fax: 020 8725 2734
Email: medicine@sghms.ac.uk
Website: www.sghms.ac.uk
Total number of students at institution: 1,500
Total number of mature students: 400

Mature Students' Officer

Phone: 020 8725 5201
Fax: 020 8725 2734
Email: medicine@sghms.ac.uk

Applications

General entry qualifications that are considered acceptable for mature applicants without the normal standard entry qualifications:

Access Course	Yes
Essay submission	No
Entrance exam	No
APEL/APL	No
Other	Foundation for medicine.

The institution does interview all mature applicants.

Funding
There are no specific mature student bursaries available over and above the national funds.

Study
Negotiated flexible learning is not available on most courses.

Timetabling hours
Lectures are timetabled between 9am and 5pm.
Modules cannot be studied that require attending only morning lectures.

Accommodation and childcare
Accommodation is available:

Specifically for mature students	No
For mature students with families	No

The institution does have crèche/childcare facilities.
Spaces are not always available.

General
There are societies or organised social activities for mature students.

College of St Mark and St John
Derriford Road
Plymouth
PL6 8BH
Phone: 01752 636890
Fax: 01752 636819
Email: admissions@marjon.ac.uk
Website: www.marjon.ac.uk

Total number of students at institution: 3060
Total number of mature students: 1010

Applications

General entry qualifications that are considered acceptable for mature applicants without the normal standard entry qualifications:

Access Course	Yes
Essay submission	No
Entrance exam	No
APEL/APL	Yes
Other	Any level three qualification will be considered.

The institution does not interview all mature applicants.

Funding

There are no specific mature student bursaries available over and above the national funds.

Study

Negotiated flexible learning is not available on most courses.

Timetabling hours

Lectures are timetabled between 9am and 5pm
Modules cannot be studied that require attending only morning lectures.

Accommodation and childcare

Accommodation is available:

Specifically for mature students	No
For mature students with families	No

The institution does have crèche/childcare facilities.
Spaces are always available.

St Mary's College

Waldergrave Road
Strawberry Hill

Twickenham
TW1 4SX
Phone: 020 8241 4000
Fax: 020 7241 2361
Email: admit@smuc.ac.uk
Website: www.smuc.ac.uk
Total number of students at institution: 2,757
Total number of mature students: 347 undergraduates

Student Support Officer
Phone: 020 8240 4139
Email: whithams@smuc.ac.uk

Applications
General entry qualifications that are considered acceptable for mature applicants without the normal standard entry qualifications:

Access Course	Yes
Essay submission	No
Entrance exam	No
APEL/APL	Yes
Other	Some study at level 3.

The institution does not interview all mature applicants.

Funding
There are no specific mature student bursaries available over and above the national funds.

Study
Negotiated flexible learning is available on some courses.
It is available to:

Full-time students	No
Part-time students	Yes
Distance Learning students	No

Timetabling hours
Lectures are timetabled between 9.00am and 7.00pm.
Modules can be studied that require attending only morning lectures.

Accommodation and childcare
Accommodation is available:

Specifically for mature students	No
For mature students with families	No

The institution does not have crèche/childcare facilities.

University of Salford
Salford
Greater Manchester
M5 4WT
Phone: 0161 295 5000
Fax: 0161 295 4704
Website: www.salford.ac.uk

Applications
General entry qualifications that are considered acceptable for mature applicants without the normal standard entry qualifications:

Access Course	Yes
Essay submission	No
Entrance exam	No
APEL/APL	Yes

The institution does not interview all mature applicants.

Salisbury College
Southampton Road
Salisbury
Wiltshire
SP1 2LW
Phone: 01722 344344
Fax: 01722 344345
Email: enquiries@salisbury.ac.uk
Website: www.salisbury.ac.uk

Applications

General entry qualifications that are considered acceptable for mature applicants without the normal standard entry qualifications:

Access Course	Yes

The institution does interview all mature applicants.

Funding

There are specific mature student bursaries available over and above the national funds.

Study

Negotiated flexible learning is available on most courses.
It is available to:

Full-time students	Yes
Part-time students	Yes
Distance Learning students	Yes
Other	Yes

Timetabling hours

Lectures are timetabled between 9am and 4pm.
Modules can be studied that require attending only morning lectures.

Accommodation and childcare

Accommodation is available:

Specifically for mature students	Yes – St Mary's hall of residence.
For mature students with families	No

The institution does have crèche/childcare facilities.
Spaces are not always available.
There are two nurseries: one at Salisbury and one at the Tidworth site.

General

There are no societies or organised social activities for mature students.

Sandwell College
Oldbury Business Centre
Pound Road
Oldbury
B68 8NA
Phone: 0121 556 6000
Fax: 0121 253 6104
Email: enquiries@sandwell.ac.uk
Website: www.sandwell.ac.uk
Total number of students at institution: 16,000
Total number of mature students: 10,500

Student Support Manager
Lesley Boyden
Phone: 0121 556 6000
Fax: 0121 253 6322
Email: lesley.boyden@sandwell.ac.uk

Applications
General entry qualifications that are considered acceptable for mature applicants without the normal standard entry qualifications:

Access Course	Yes
Entrance exam	No
APEL/APL	Yes
Other	Interview and/or portfolio.

The institution does interview all mature applicants.

Funding
There are no specific mature student bursaries available over and above the national funds.

Study
Negotiated flexible learning is not available on most courses.

Timetabling hours
Modules cannot be studied that require attending only morning lectures.

Accommodation and childcare
Accommodation is available:

Specifically for mature students	Yes

The institution does have crèche/childcare facilities.
There are 90 spaces.
Spaces are not always available.
Access to a list of registered childcare providers in the area is available.

General
There are no societies or organised social activities specifically for mature students.

Sheffield College
HE Unit
PO Box 730
Sheffield
S6 5YF
Phone: 0114 260 2216
Fax: 0114 260 2282
Email: heunit@sheffcol.ac.uk
Website: www.sheffcol.ac.uk
Total number of students at institution: 26,000
Total number of mature students: 18,000

Student Support
Phone numbers:
Castle site: 0114 260 2102
Loxley site: 0114 260 2202
Norton site: 0114 260 2302
Parson Cross site: 0114 260 2502

Student Financial Support Officer
Mr C. Marriott
Phone: 0114 260 2600
Email: christian.marriott@sheffcol.ac.uk

Applications
General entry qualifications that are considered acceptable for mature applicants without the normal standard entry qualifications:

Access Course	Yes
Essay submission	No
Entrance exam	No
APEL/APL	Yes

The institution does interview all mature applicants.

Study

Negotiated flexible learning is available on most courses.
It is available to:

Full-time students	No
Part-time students	Yes
Distance Learning students	Yes
Other	Some online courses are available.

Timetabling hours

Lectures are timetabled between 9am and 9pm.
Modules can be studied that require attending only morning lectures.

Accommodation and childcare

Accommodation is available:

Specifically for mature students	Yes – accommodation through Sheffield Hallam University Accommodation Services.
For mature students with families	No

The institution does have crèche/childcare facilities.
There are 154 spaces.
Spaces are not always available.
Help is available to source other childcare facilities.

General

There are some organised social activities for students.

University of Sheffield
Firth Court
Western Bank
Sheffield
S10 2TN
Phone: 0114 222 2000
Website: www.sheffield.ac.uk
Total number of students at institution: c.16,000 (full-time)
Total number of mature students: c.1,100 (full-time)

Mature Students' Officer
Phone: 0114 222 8035
Fax: 0114 222 1234
Email: mature.student@sheffield.ac.uk

Student Services Information Desk
Phone: 0114 2221316/8660
Email: advice@sheffield.ac.uk

Applications
General entry qualifications that are considered acceptable for mature
applicants without the normal standard entry qualifications:

Access Course	Yes
Other	Life experience may be appropriate: contact the relevant department.

The institution does not interview all mature applicants.

Funding
There are no specific mature student bursaries available over and above the
national funds.

Study
Negotiated flexible learning is available on some courses.

Timetabling hours

Lecture times vary according to course.

Accommodation and childcare

Accommodation is available:

Specifically for mature students	Yes – shared housing with other mature students. See www.sheffield.ac.uk/housing/apply.html.
For mature students with families	Yes – there are a number of flats available that are suitable for families.

The institution does have crèche/childcare facilities.
Spaces are not always available.
Apply to Cilla Carr of the Students' Union at nursery@sheffield.ac.uk

General

There are societies or organised social activities for mature students.
These are organised by the mature student committee
(msc@sheffield.ac.uk).
There is online information specifically for mature students at
www.shef.ac.uk/rao/recruitment/mature/, and there will be a mature student
guide from November 2004.

Sheffield Hallam University

City Campus
Howard Street
Sheffield
S1 1WB
Phone: 0114 225 5555
Fax: 0114 225 2094
Website: www.shu.ac.uk

Mature Students' Officer

Annette Sundaraj
Phone: 0114 225 4986
Fax: 0114 225 2046
Email: a.sundaraj@shu.ac.uk

Applications

General entry qualifications that are considered acceptable for mature applicants without the normal standard entry qualifications:

Access Course	Yes
APEL/APL	Yes
Other	Exam or essay (very rarely).

The institution does not interview all mature applicants.

Funding

There are no specific mature student bursaries available over and above the national funds.

Study

Negotiated flexible learning is available on most courses.
It is available to:

Full-time students	Yes
Part-time students	Yes
Distance Learning students	Yes

Timetabling hours

Lectures are timetabled between 9am and 9pm.
Modules cannot be studied that require attending only morning lectures.

Accommodation and childcare

Accommodation is available:

Specifically for mature students	No

The institution does have crèche/childcare facilities.

General
There are no societies or organised social activities for mature students.
There is online information specifically for mature students.

Shrewsbury College of Arts and Technology
London Road
Shrewsbury
Shropshire
SY2 6PR
Phone: 01743 342342
Fax: 01743 342343
Email: prospects@shrewsbury.ac.uk
Website: www.shrewsbury.ac.uk

Mature Students' Officer
John Morris
Phone: 01743 342321
Fax: 01743 342343
Email: johnm@shrewsbury.ac.uk

Student Support Officer
Matt James
Phone: 01743 342342
Fax: 01743 342343
Email: matthewj@shrewsbury.ac.uk

Applications
General entry qualifications that are considered acceptable for mature
applicants without the normal standard entry qualifications:

Access Course	Yes
APEL/APL	Yes

The institution does interview all mature applicants.

Funding
There are specific mature student bursaries available over and above the
national funds.

Study

Negotiated flexible learning is available on some courses.
It is available to:

Full-time students	No
Part-time students	Yes
Distance Learning students	Yes

Timetabling hours

Lectures are timetabled between 9am and 9pm.
Modules can be studied that require attending only morning lectures.

Accommodation and childcare

Accommodation is available:

Specifically for mature students	No
For mature students with families	No

The institution does have crèche/childcare facilities.
Spaces are not always available.

General

There are no societies or organised social activities for mature students.

School of Oriental and African Studies

Thornhaugh Street
Russell Square
London
WC1H 0XG
Phone: 020 7637 2388
Fax: 020 7898 4039
Email: study@soas.ac.uk
Website: www.soas.ac.uk
Total number of students at institution: 3,284
Total number of mature students: 1,313

Mature Students' Officer

Phone: 020 7898 4996
Fax: 020 7436 3844
Email: mature@soas.ac.uk

Student Support Officers
Judith Barnett/Heather McLeod
Phone: 020 7074 5014
Fax: 020 7074 5039
Email: jb25@soas.ac.uk or hm18@soas.ac.uk

Applications
General entry qualifications that are considered acceptable for mature applicants without the normal standard entry qualifications:

Access Course	Yes

The institution does not interview all mature applicants.

Funding
There are no specific mature student bursaries available over and above the national funds.

Study
Negotiated flexible learning is not available on most courses.

Timetabling hours
Lectures are timetabled between 9am and 5pm.
Modules can be studied that require attending only morning lectures.

Accommodation and childcare
Accommodation is available:

Specifically for mature students	No
For mature students with families	Yes – some double rooms are available.

The institution does not have crèche/childcare facilities.

General
There are societies or organised social activities for mature students.
Events include the mature students' orientation week.
There is online information specifically for mature students without formal qualifications.

School of Pharmacy

29–39 Brunswick Square
London
WC1N 1AX
Phone: 020 7753 5831
Fax: 020 7753 5829
Email: registry@ulsop.ac.uk
Website: www.ulsop.ac.uk
Total number of students at institution: 670 undergraduates
Total number of mature students: 135 undergraduates

Student Support Officer

Phone: 020 7753 5831
Fax: 020 7753 5829
Email: registry@ulsop.ac.uk

Applications

Please contact the School for information about entry qualifications that
are considered acceptable for mature applicants without the normal
standard entry qualifications.
The institution does interview all mature applicants with non-standard
qualifications.

Funding

There are no specific mature student bursaries available over and above the
national funds, but hardship funds are available.

Study

Negotiated flexible learning is not available on most courses.

Timetabling hours

Lectures are timetabled between 9.00am and 6.00pm.
Modules cannot be studied that require attending only morning lectures.

Accommodation and childcare

Accommodation is available:

Specifically for mature students	Yes
For mature students with families	Yes

The institution does not have crèche/childcare facilities.

General

There are no societies or organised social activities for mature students. The professional nature of the Pharmacy degree attracts a large number of mature students to the course.

South Devon College

Newton Road
Torquay
South Devon
Phone: 01803 400700
Fax: 01803 400701
Email: courses@southdevon.ac.uk
Website: www.southdevon.ac.uk
Total number of students at institution: 8,748
Total number of mature students: 7,179

Admissions Officer

Dot Swann
Phone: 01803 406405
Fax: 01803 400701
Email: dswann@southdevon.ac.uk

Student Services Manager

Gordon Budd
Phone: 01803 406242
Fax: 01803 400701
Email: gbudd@southdevon.ac.uk

Applications

General entry qualifications that are considered acceptable for mature applicants without the normal standard entry qualifications:

Access Course	Yes
Essay submission	Yes
Entrance exam	Yes

The institution does interview all mature applicants.

Funding

There are no specific mature student bursaries available over and above the national funds.

Study

Negotiated flexible learning is only available to distance learning students.

Timetabling hours

Modules can be studied that require attending only morning lectures.

Accommodation and childcare

Accommodation is available:

Specifically for mature students	No
For mature students with families	No

The institution does have crèche/childcare facilities.
Spaces are not always available, but needs can usually be accommodated.

General

There are societies and organised social activities but not specifically for mature students.

South East Essex College

Carnarvon Road
Southend-on-Sea
Essex
SS2 6LS
Phone: 01702 220400
Fax: 01702 432320
Email: marketing@southend.ac.uk
Website: www.southend.ac.uk
Total number of students at institution: 8,102
Total number of mature students: 4,602

Student Support Officer

Georgina Murrell
Phone: 01702 220400
Fax: 01702 432320
Email: marketing@southend.ac.uk

Applications

General entry qualifications that are considered acceptable for mature applicants without the normal standard entry qualifications:

Access Course	Yes

The institution does interview all mature applicants.

Funding

There are no specific mature student bursaries available over and above the national funds.

Study

Negotiated flexible learning is available on most courses.
It is available to:

Full-time students	No
Part-time students	Yes
Distance Learning students	Yes

Timetabling hours

Lectures are timetabled between 9am and 9pm.
Modules cannot be studied that require attending only morning lectures.

Accommodation and childcare

Accommodation is available:

Specifically for mature students	No – all accommodation is in the private sector. We endeavour to help students secure housing through the accommodation scheme.
For mature students with families	No

The institution does have crèche/childcare facilities.

Spaces are not always available.

There is a waiting list for spaces.

The Jungle Cats nursery is available to student parents.

General

There are no societies or organised social activities for mature students, but there is a forum for all HE students, including mature students.

South Nottingham College

West Bridgford Centre
Greythorn Drive
West Bridgford
Nottingham
NG2 7GA
Phone: 0115 914 6400
Fax: 0115 914 6444
Email: enquiries@south-nottingham.ac.uk
Website: www.south-nottingham.ac.uk
Total number of students at institution: 24,000 (part-time and full-time)

Applications

The institution does interview all mature applicants.

Funding

There are no specific mature student bursaries available over and above the national funds.

Study

Negotiated flexible learning is not available on most courses.

Timetabling hours

Modules cannot be studied that require attending only morning lectures.

Accommodation and childcare

Accommodation is available:

Specifically for mature students	No – institution will work to individual needs.

For mature students with families	No – institution will work to individual needs.

The institution does have crèche/childcare facilities.
Spaces are usually available.

General

There are no societies or organised social activities for mature students.
There is no online information specifically for mature students.
Applications are dealt with on an individual basis.

University of Southampton

University Road
Highfield
Southampton
SO17 1BJ
Phone: 023 8059 5000
Website: www.soton.ac.uk
Total number of students at institution: 19,000

Student Support Officer

Theresa McGoldrick
Fax: 023 8059 3062
Email: 023 8059 3037

Applications

General entry qualifications that are considered acceptable for mature
applicants without the normal standard entry qualifications vary from
discipline to discipline, i.e. there might be APEL/APL and/or interview.

Funding

There are no specific mature student bursaries available over and above the
national funds.

Study

Negotiated flexible learning is only available on some distance learning
courses; it is not widespread.

Timetabling hours
Lectures are timetabled between 9am and 5.30pm.

Accommodation and childcare
Accommodation is available:

Specifically for mature students	Yes – apply to accommodation office.
For mature students with families	Yes – apply to accommodation office.

The institution does have crèche/childcare facilities.
There are 108 spaces.
Apply to the manager of the day nursery.

General
There are no societies or organised social activities for mature students.

Southampton City College
St Mary Street
Southampton
SO14 1AR
Phone: 023 8048 4848
Fax: 023 8057 7374
Email: information@southampton-city.ac.uk
Website: www.southampton-city.ac.uk
Total number of students at institution: 10,500
Total number of mature students: 9,000

Student Support Officer
Miranda Shoebridge
Phone: 023 8057 7379
Fax: 023 8057 7374
Email: miranda.shoebridge@southampton-city.ac.uk

Applications
General entry qualifications that are considered acceptable for mature
applicants without the normal standard entry qualifications:

Access Course	Yes
Essay submission	Yes – sometimes
Entrance exam	No
Other	Interview and initial assessment.

The institution does interview all mature applicants for full-time courses.

Funding
There are no specific mature student bursaries available over and above the national funds.

Timetabling hours
Lectures are timetabled between 9.00am and 9.00pm.
Depending on the course, modules can be studied that require attending only morning lectures.

Accommodation and childcare
Accommodation is available:

Specifically for mature students	No
For mature students with families	No

The institution does have crèche/childcare facilities.
There are 82 spaces.
Spaces are not always available.
Childminders are funded.

General
There are no societies or organised social activities for mature students.
There is no online information specifically for mature students.

Southwark College
The Cut
Waterloo
London
SE1 8LE
Phone: 020 7815 1600
Fax: 020 7261 1301
Website: www.southwark.ac.uk

Student Support Officer
Ciara Bomford
Phone: 020 7815 1605
Fax: 020 7261 1301
Email: ciarab@southwark.ac.uk

Applications
General entry qualifications that are considered acceptable for mature applicants without the normal standard entry qualifications:

Entrance exam	Yes

The institution does interview all mature applicants.

Funding
There are no specific mature student bursaries available over and above the national funds.

Study
Negotiated flexible learning is available to distance learning students.

Timetabling hours
Modules can be studied that require attending only morning lectures.

Accommodation and childcare
Accommodation is available:

Specifically for mature students	No
For mature students with families	No

The institution does have crèche/childcare facilities.

General
There are societies or organised social activities for mature students.

Spurgeon's College
189 South Norwood Hill
London
SE25 6DJ
Phone: 020 8653 0850

Fax: 020 8771 0959
Email: enquiries@spurgeons.ac.uk
Website: www.spurgeons.ac.uk
Total number of students at institution: 350
Total number of mature students: 350

Student Support Officer

Paul Scott-Evans
Phone: 020 8653 0850

Applications

General entry qualifications that are considered acceptable for mature
applicants without the normal standard entry qualifications:

Other	Ability to complete the course.

The institution does interview all mature applicants.

Funding

There are specific mature student bursaries available over and above the
national funds.

Study

Negotiated flexible learning is available on most courses.
It is available to:

Full-time students	Yes
Part-time students	Yes
Distance Learning students	Yes

Timetabling hours

Lectures are timetabled between 8.30am and 4pm.
Modules cannot be studied that require attending only morning lectures.

Accommodation and childcare

Accommodation is available:

Specifically for mature students	Yes
For mature students with families	Yes – one- and two-bedroom flats are available.

The institution does not have crèche/childcare facilities.

General
There are societies or organised social activities for mature students.

Staffordshire University
College Road
Stoke-on-Trent
ST4 2DE
Phone: 01782 292746
Email: admissions@staffs.ac.uk
Website: www.staffs.ac.uk

Student Support Officer
Phone: 01782 292746

Applications
General entry qualifications that are considered acceptable for mature applicants without the normal standard entry qualifications:

Access Course	Yes
Essay submission	Yes
Entrance exam	No
APEL/APL	Yes

The institution does not interview all mature applicants.

Funding
There are no specific mature student bursaries available over and above the national funds.

Study
Negotiated flexible learning is available on some courses, but only at postgraduate level.
It is available to:

Full-time students	No
Part-time students	Yes
Distance Learning students	Yes

Timetabling hours

Undergraduate full-time lectures are timetabled between 9am and 6pm. Modules cannot be studied that require attending only morning lectures.

Accommodation and childcare

Accommodation is available:

Specifically for mature students	No
For mature students with families	No

The institution does have crèche/childcare facilities.
There are 67 spaces.
Spaces are not always available.

General

There are societies or organised social activities for mature students, such as the focus group lunch. Mature students can organise a society through the students' union.
There is online information for mature students at www.staffs.ac.uk/heshop

---

University of Stirling

Stirling
FK9 4LA
Phone: 01786 467046
Fax: 01786 466800
Email: recruitment@stir.ac.uk
Website: www.stir.ac.uk
Total number of students at institution: 8,000
Total number of mature students: 1,200 (15 per cent of full-time students)

Student Information and Support Service

Phone: 01786 467080
Email: siss1@stir.ac.uk

Applications

General entry qualifications that are considered acceptable for mature applicants without the normal standard entry qualifications:

Access Course	Yes
APEL/APL	Yes

The institution does not interview all mature applicants.

Funding
There are no specific mature student bursaries available over and above the national funds.

Study
Negotiated flexible learning is only available to part-time students on some courses.

Timetabling hours
Lectures are timetabled between 9am and 6pm (daytime lectures) and between 6pm and 9pm (evening lectures).

Accommodation and childcare
Accommodation is available:

For mature students with families	Yes – limited number available.

The institution does not have crèche/childcare facilities but there is a nursery by the campus entrance.

General
The mature students' society organises social activities for mature students. There is a mature students' leaflet available. Contact the admissions or recruitment office for a copy to be sent.

Stockport College of Further and Higher Education
Wellington Road South
Stockport
SK1 3UQ
Phone: 0161 958 3100
Email: enquiries@stockport.ac.uk
Website: www.stockport.ac.uk
Total number of students at institution: 10,390
Total number of mature students: 7,490

Student Support Officer

Jacquie Campbell
Phone: 0161 958 3142
Fax: 0161 958 3384
Email: enquiries@stockport.ac.uk

Applications

General entry qualifications that are considered acceptable for mature
applicants without the normal standard entry qualifications:

Access Course	Yes
Essay submission	No
Entrance exam	No
APEL/APL	Yes

The institution does not interview all mature applicants.

Funding

There are no specific mature student bursaries available over and above the
national funds.

Study

Negotiated flexible learning is not available on most courses.
Distance learning is available.

Timetabling hours

Modules cannot be studied that require attending only morning lectures.

Accommodation and childcare

Accommodation is available:

Specifically for mature students	No
For mature students with families	No

The institution does have crèche/childcare facilities.
There are 20 full-time spaces.
Spaces are not always available.

General

There are no societies or organised social activities for mature students.

Stoke on Trent College

Stoke Road
Shelton
Stoke on Trent
Staffordshire
ST4 2DG
Phone: 01782 208208
Fax: 01782 603504
Email: info@stokecoll.ac.uk
Website: www.stokecoll.ac.uk
Total number of students at institution: 30,000
Total number of mature students: 25,000

Student Support Officer

Francesca Coxon
Phone: 01782 208208 ext. 3279
Email: fcoxolsc@stokecoll.ac.uk

Applications

General entry qualifications that are considered acceptable for mature applicants without the normal standard entry qualifications:

Access Course	Yes
Essay submission	Yes
Entrance exam	Yes

Funding

There are no specific mature student bursaries available over and above the national funds.

Study

Negotiated flexible learning is not available on most courses.

Timetabling hours

Modules can be studied that require attending only morning lectures.

Accommodation and childcare

Accommodation is available:

Specifically for mature students	No
For mature students with families	No

The institution does have crèche/childcare facilities.
Spaces are not always available.

General

There are no societies or organised social activities for mature students.
There is no online information specifically for mature students.

Stranmillis University College

Stranmillis Road
Belfast
BT9 5DY
Phone: 028 9038 1291
Fax: 028 9066 4423
Email: registry@stran.ac.uk
Website: www.stran.ac.uk
Total number of students at institution: 1,200
Total number of mature students: 120

Mature Students' Officer

M. Watson
Phone: 028 9038 1291

Student Support Officer

Dr B. Erwin
Phone: 028 9038 1291

Applications

General entry qualifications that are considered acceptable for mature
applicants without the normal standard entry qualifications:

Access Course	Yes
APEL/APL	Yes

The institution does interview all mature applicants.

Funding

There are no specific mature student bursaries available over and above the
national funds.

Study

Negotiated flexible learning is available to part-time students.

Timetabling hours

Lectures are timetabled between 9am and 8pm.
Modules can be studied that require attending only morning lectures.

Accommodation and childcare

Accommodation is available:

Specifically for mature students	No
For mature students with families	No

The institution does not have crèche/childcare facilities.

General

There are societies or organised social activities for mature students.

University of Strathclyde

Richmond Street
Glasgow
Phone: 0141 548 4248
Fax: 0141 552 7362
Email: ais@mis.strath.ac.uk
Website: www.strath.ac.uk
Total number of students at institution: 14,563
Total number of mature students: 2,039 (i.e. 14 per cent)

Mature Students' Officer

Phone: 0141 548 4248
Fax: 0141 552 7362
Email: ais@mis.strath.ac.uk

Applications

General entry qualifications that are considered acceptable for mature
applicants without the normal standard entry qualifications:

Access Course	Yes
Essay submission	Yes
Entrance exam	Yes
APEL/APL	Yes

The institution does not interview all mature applicants.

Funding
There are specific mature student bursaries available over and above the national funds.

Study
Negotiated flexible learning is not available on most courses.

Timetabling hours
Lectures are timetabled between 9.00am and 5.00pm.
Modules cannot be studied that require attending only morning lectures.

Accommodation and childcare
Accommodation is available:

Specifically for mature students	No
For mature students with families	No

The institution does have crèche/childcare facilities.
Spaces are not always available.
There is also an October break crèche.

General
There are societies or organised social activities for mature students. There is a Mature Students' Association.
There is online information specifically for mature students at www.strath.ac.uk
A Mature Student Guide is available on request.

University of Sunderland
Langham Tower
Ryhope Road
Sunderland
SR2 7EE
Phone: 0191 515 2000
Fax: 0191 515 3805
Email: student-helpline@sunderland.ac.uk
Website: www.sunderland.ac.uk
Total number of students at institution: 18,537
Total number of mature students: 12,542

Mature Students' Officer

Phone: 0191 515 3000
Fax: 0191 515 3805
Email: student-helpline@sunderland.ac.uk

Applications

General entry qualifications that are considered acceptable for mature
applicants without the normal standard entry qualifications:

Access Course	Yes
APEL/APL	Yes
Other	Yes – depending on the course.

The institution does not interview all mature applicants.

Funding

There are no specific mature student bursaries available over and above the
national funds.

Study

Negotiated flexible learning is only available to distance learning students.

Timetabling hours

Lectures are timetabled between 9am and 9pm.
Modules can be studied that require attending only morning lectures.

Accommodation and childcare

Accommodation is available:
Specifically for mature students Yes – separate block of accommodation and
specific flats. For mature students with families Yes – there are family
provisions.
The institution does have crèche/childcare facilities.
Number of spaces depends on age of child.
Spaces are always available.

General

The mature students' society organises social activities for mature students.
There is online information specifically for mature students. As the visitor
to the website inputs their age, tailored web pages are activated, which are
specific to the age group and information required.

The University of Sunderland welcomes applications from mature students and they are considered on an individual basis.

Surrey Institute of Art and Design University College

Falkner Road
Farnham
Surrey
GU9 7DS
Phone: 01252 722441
Fax: 01252 733869
Email: registry@surrart.ac.uk
Website: www.surrart.ac.uk

Welfare Services Officer

Phone: 01252 892612
Fax: 01252 892623
Email: rsykes@surrart.ac.uk

Applications

General entry qualifications that are considered acceptable for mature applicants without the normal standard entry qualifications:

Access Course	Yes
Essay submission	No
Entrance exam	No
APEL/APL	Yes
Other	A-levels or other evidence of ability.

Funding

There are no specific mature student bursaries available over and above the national funds.

Study

Negotiated flexible learning is not available on most courses.

Timetabling hours

Lectures are timetabled between 9am and 5pm for full-time students, and part-time students attend two days a week.

Accommodation and childcare
Accommodation is available:

Specifically for mature students	No
For mature students with families	No

The institution does not have crèche/childcare facilities.

General
There are no societies or organised social activities for mature students.

University of Surrey Roehampton
Erasmus House
Roehampton Lane
London
SW15 5PU
Phone: 020 8392 3000
Fax: 020 8392 3470
Email: enquiries@roehampton.ac.uk
Website: www.roehampton.ac.uk/prospectus
Total number of students at institution: 7,309
Total number of mature students: 1,700

Mature Students' Officer
Phone: 020 8392 3221
Fax: 020 8392 3287
Email: d.howley@roehampton.ac.uk

Applications
General entry qualifications that are considered acceptable for mature applicants without the normal standard entry qualifications:

Access Course	Yes
APEL/APL	Yes
Other	Interview

The institution does not interview all mature applicants.

Funding

There are specific mature student bursaries available over and above the national funds.

Study

Negotiated flexible learning may be available, depending on the course.

Timetabling hours

Lectures are timetabled between 9am and 7.30pm.
Modules can be studied that require attending only morning lectures.

Accommodation and childcare

Accommodation is available:

Specifically for mature students	Yes
For mature students with families	No

The institution does have crèche/childcare facilities.
Spaces are not always available.

General

There are societies or organised social activities for mature students.
There is online information specifically for mature students.
Roehampton's RED centre offers sensitive academic support. There is also a counselling service if required.

University of Sussex

Falmer
Brighton
East Sussex
BN1 9RH
Phone: 01273 606755
Fax: 01273 678545
Email: information@sussex.ac.uk
Website: www.sussex.ac.uk
Total number of undergraduate students at institution: 7,091
Total number of mature students: 1,645

Mature Students' Officer

Phone: 01273 678416

Fax: 01273 678545

Email: ug.admissions@sussex.ac.uk

Head of Student Support

Sue Yates

Phone: 01273 678222

Fax: 01273 877366

Email: s.m.yates@sussex.ac.uk

Applications

General entry qualifications that are considered acceptable for mature applicants without the normal standard entry qualifications:

Access Course	Yes
Essay submission	Yes
Entrance exam	No
APEL/APL	Yes

The institution does not interview all mature applicants.

Funding

There are specific mature student bursaries available over and above the national funds.

Study

Negotiated flexible learning is not available on most courses.

Timetabling hours

Lectures are timetabled between 9am to 6pm.

Accommodation and childcare

Accommodation is available:

Specifically for mature students	Yes – Norwich House is a designated mature and international student house.

For mature students with families	Yes – 70 small family flats available, mostly on campus.

The institution does have crèche/childcare facilities.

There are 43 spaces for children aged 3 years and under, and 40 spaces for 3–5-year-olds.

Spaces are not always available. Places are oversubscribed – apply early.

There is also a students' union playgroup and an after-school club.

General

There are societies or organised social activities for mature students.

These are organised by the mature students' society and the parents' group.

There is online information specifically for mature students at

http://www.sussex.ac.uk/Units/publications/ugrad2004/1-4-1.html

The prospectus, which is also online, has a mature student section.

Sutton Coldfield College

Lichfield Road

Sutton Coldfield

West Midlands

B74 2NW

Phone: 0121 355 5671

Fax: 0121 362 1150

Email: adulted@sutcol.ac.uk

Website: www.sutcol.ac.uk

Applications

General entry qualifications that are considered acceptable for mature applicants without the normal standard entry qualifications:

Access Course	Yes
APEL/APL	Yes

The institution does interview all mature applicants.

Funding

There are no specific mature student bursaries available over and above the national funds.

Study

Negotiated flexible learning is not available on most courses.

Timetabling hours

Lectures are timetabled between 10am and 3pm.
Modules cannot be studied that require attending only morning lectures.

Accommodation and childcare

Accommodation is available:

Specifically for mature students	Yes
For mature students with families	No

The institution does have crèche/childcare facilities.

General

There are no societies or organised social activities for mature students.

Swindon College

Regent Circus
Swindon
SN1 1PT
Phone: 01793 491591
Fax: 01793 641794
Email: adviceandguidance@swindon-college.ac.uk
Website: www.swindon-college.ac.uk

Applications

General entry qualifications that are considered acceptable for mature applicants without the normal standard entry qualifications:

Access Course	Yes
Essay submission	No
Entrance exam	No
APEL/APL	Yes
Other	Relevant experience.

The institution does interview all mature applicants.

Funding

There are specific mature student bursaries available over and above the national funds. There is an access fund available.

Study

Negotiated flexible learning is available on most courses.
It is available to:

Full-time students	Yes
Part-time students	Yes
Distance Learning students	Yes

Timetabling hours

Lectures are timetabled between 9am and 9pm.
Modules cannot be studied that require attending only morning lectures.

Accommodation and childcare

Accommodation is available:

Specifically for mature students	No
For mature students with families	No

The institution does have crèche/childcare facilities.
Spaces are not always available and are subject to demand.

General

There are no societies or organised social activities for mature students.

Tameside College

Ashton Centre
Beaufort Road
Ashton-under-Lyne
OL6 6NX
Phone: 0161 908 6600
Fax: 0161 908 6611
Website: www.tameside.ac.uk
Total number of students at institution: 9,079
Total number of mature students: 5,702

Mature Students' Officer
Phone: 0161 908 6789
Fax: 0161 908 6749

Student Service Adviser
Phone: 0161 908 6789
Fax: 0161 908 6749

Applications
General entry qualifications that are considered acceptable for mature
applicants without the normal standard entry qualifications:

Access Course	Yes
Essay submission	Yes
Entrance exam	Yes
APEL/APL	Yes
Other	Personal statement, reference, interview screening.

The institution does interview all full-time and some part-time mature
applicants.

Funding
There are no specific mature student bursaries available over and above the
national funds.

Study
Negotiated flexible learning is available.
It is available to:

Full-time students	Yes – on some courses.
Part-time students	Yes – on some courses.
Distance Learning students	Yes

Timetabling hours

Lectures are timetabled between 9am and 9pm.

Modules cannot be studied that require attending only morning lectures.

Accommodation and childcare

Accommodation is available:

Specifically for mature students	Yes – there is a student accommodation database.
For mature students with families	Yes – there is a student accommodation database.

The institution does have crèche/childcare facilities.

Spaces are not always available; the facility operates on a 'first come, first served' basis at the beginning of term.

Details of the childcare scheme are available on request.

General

There are societies or organised social activities for mature students.

There is online information specifically for mature students on the 'adult opportunities' page.

Tamworth and Lichfield College

Croft Street
Upper Gungate
Tamworth
Staffordshire
Phone: 01827 310202
Fax: 01827 59437
Email: enquiries@tamworth.ac.uk
Website: www.tlc.ac.uk
Total number of students at institution: 650 (both full-time and part-time)

Student Support Officer

Margaret Youlden

Phone: 01827 310202

Fax: 01827 59437

Applications

General entry qualifications that are considered acceptable for mature applicants without the normal standard entry qualifications:

Access Course	Yes
Essay submission	No
Entrance exam	No
APEL/APL	Yes

The institution does not interview all mature applicants.

Funding

There are no specific mature student bursaries available over and above the national funds.

Study

Negotiated flexible learning is not available on most courses.

Timetabling hours

Lectures are timetabled between 9am and 9pm.

Modules can be studied that require attending only morning lectures.

Accommodation and childcare

Accommodation is available:

Specifically for mature students	No
For mature students with families	No

The institution does have crèche/childcare facilities.

Spaces are not always available.

General

There are no societies or organised social activities for mature students.

Thames Valley University

St Mary's Road
Ealing
London
W5 5RF
Phone: 0800 036 8888
Fax: 020 8231 2056
Email: learning.advice@tvu.ac.uk
Website: www.tvu.ac.uk
Total number of students at institution: 23,414

Student Advice Team

Phone: 020 8231 2573
Fax: 020 8231 2587
Email: student.advice@tvu.ac.uk

Applications

General entry qualifications that are considered acceptable for mature
applicants without the normal standard entry qualifications:

Access Course	Yes
APEL/APL	Yes

Funding

There are no specific mature student bursaries available over and above the
national funds.

Study

Negotiated flexible learning is available on some courses.

Accommodation and childcare

Accommodation is available:

Specifically for mature students	No
For mature students with families	No

The institution does not have crèche/childcare facilities.
Students may be helped with childcare costs through the Access to
Learning Fund.

Thomas Danby College

Roundhay Road
Leeds
West Yorkshire
LS7 3BG
Phone: 0800 096 2319/0113 249 4912
Fax: 0113 240 1967
Email: info@thomasdanby.ac.uk
Website: www.thomasdanby.ac.uk
Total number of students at institution: 15,685
Total number of mature students: 8,784 (over 19 years of age)

Guidance Service

Steven Bone
Phone: 0113 240 1967

Applications

General entry qualifications that are considered acceptable for mature applicants without the normal standard entry qualifications:

Access Course	Yes
Essay submission	Yes
Entrance exam	Yes
APEL/APL	Yes

Funding

There are no specific mature student bursaries available over and above the national funds.

Study

Negotiated flexible learning is available on some courses.
It is available to:

Full-time students	No
Part-time students	Yes
Distance Learning students	Yes

Timetabling hours

Lectures are timetabled between 9am and 9pm.

Accommodation and childcare

Accommodation is available:

Specifically for mature students	No
For mature students with families	No

The institution does have crèche/childcare facilities.
There are 50 spaces.
Spaces are not always available.

General

There are societies or organised social activities for mature students.
There is online information specifically for mature students.

Totton College

Water Lane
Totton
Hants
SO40 3ZX
Phone: 023 8087 4874
Fax: 023 80874879
Email: info@totton.ac.uk
Website: www.totton.ac.uk

Mature Students' Officer

Phone: 023 8087 4688
Fax: 023 8087 4879
Email: rpenny@totton.ac.uk

Student Support Officer

June Crump
Phone: 023 8087 4888
Fax: 023 8087 4879
Email: jcrump@totton.ac.uk

Applications

General entry qualifications that are considered acceptable for mature
applicants without the normal standard entry qualifications:

Access Course	Yes
Essay submission	Yes
APEL/APL	Yes

The institution does interview all mature applicants.

Funding

There are no specific mature student bursaries available over and above the national funds.

Study

Negotiated flexible learning is available on most courses.
It is available to:

Full-time students	Yes
Part-time students	Yes

Timetabling hours

Lectures are timetabled between 9.00am and 8.00pm.
Modules can be studied that require attending only morning lectures.

Accommodation and childcare

Accommodation is available:

Specifically for mature students	No
For mature students with families	No

The institution does have crèche/childcare facilities.
Spaces are not always available.

General

There are no societies or organised social activities for mature students.
The College offers foundation degrees in partnership with Southampton University.

Trinity College

College Road
Carmarthen
SA31 3EP

Phone: 01276 676767
Fax: 01267 676766
Email: registry@trinity-cm.ac.uk
Website: www.trinity-cm.ac.uk
Total number of students at institution: 3,386
Total number of mature students: 1,996

Student Services

Phone: 01267 676825
Fax: 01267 676766

Applications

General entry qualifications that are considered acceptable for mature
applicants without the normal standard entry qualifications:

Access Course	Yes
Entrance exam	No
APEL/APL	Yes

The institution does not interview all mature applicants.

Funding

There are no specific mature student bursaries available over and above the
national funds.

Study

Negotiated flexible learning is not available on most courses.
It is available to:

Full-time students	Yes
Part-time students	Yes
Distance Learning students	Yes

Timetabling hours

Lectures are timetabled between 9.15am and 4.15pm.

Accommodation and childcare

Accommodation is available:

Specifically for mature students	No
For mature students with families	No

The institution does have crèche/childcare facilities.
Spaces are not always available.

General
There are societies or organised social activities for mature students.

Wakefield College
Margaret Street
Wakefield
West Yorkshire
WF1 2DH
Phone: 01924 789299
Fax: 01924 789380
Email: courseinfo@wakcoll.ac.uk
Website: www.wakcoll.ac.uk
Total number of students at institution: 12,000
Total number of mature students: 8,000

Mature Students' Officer
Phone: 01924 789299
Fax: 01924 789380
Email: p.millner@wakcoll.ac.uk

Applications
General entry qualifications that are considered acceptable for mature
applicants without the normal standard entry qualifications:

Access Course	Yes
Essay submission	Yes
Entrance exam	No
APEL/APL	Yes

The institution does interview all mature applicants.

Funding
There are no specific mature student bursaries available over and above the
national funds.

Study
Negotiated flexible learning is available on some courses.

It is available to:

Full-time students	Yes
Part-time students	Yes
Distance Learning students	No

Timetabling hours
Lectures are timetabled between 9am and 9pm.
Modules can be studied that require attending only morning lectures.

Accommodation and childcare
Accommodation is available:

Specifically for mature students	No
For mature students with families	No

The institution does have crèche/childcare facilities.
There are 30 spaces.
Spaces are not always available.

General
There are no societies or organised social activities for mature students.

University of Wales, Bangor
(Prifysgol Cymru, Bangor)
Bangor
Gwynedd
LL57 2DG
Phone: 01248 351151
Website: www.bangor.ac.uk
Total number of students at institution: 8,000
Total number of mature students: 1,500–2,000

Student Support Officer
Steph Barbaresi
Phone: 01248 382023
Fax: 01248 383588

Applications

General entry qualifications that are considered acceptable for mature applicants without the normal standard entry qualifications:

Access Course	Yes
Essay submission	Yes
APEL/APL	Yes

The institution does not interview all mature applicants.

Funding

There are specific mature student bursaries available over and above the national funds.

Study

Negotiated flexible learning is available on most courses.
It is available to:

Full-time students	Yes
Part-time students	Yes
Distance Learning students	Yes

Timetabling hours

Lectures are timetabled between 8.30am and 6pm.
Modules can be studied that require attending only morning lectures.

Accommodation and childcare

Accommodation is available:

Specifically for mature students	Yes – there is a hall for mature students.
For mature students with families	Yes – there are family flats and houses.

The institution does have crèche/childcare facilities.
There are 50 spaces.
Spaces are not always available.

General

The mature student association organises social activities for mature students.

There is a booklet of information specifically for mature students.

University of Wales College of Medicine

Heath Park
Cardiff
CF14 4XN
Phone: 029 2074 7747
Website: www.uwcm.ac.uk
Total number of students at institution: 3,500

Student Support Officer

Phone: 029 2074 2070
Email: sss@cf.ac.uk

Applications

General entry qualifications that are considered acceptable for mature applicants without the normal standard entry qualifications:

Access Course	Yes	
Essay submission Yes APEL/APL	Yes	

The institution does interview all mature applicants.

Funding

There are no specific mature student bursaries available over and above the national funds.

Study

Negotiated flexible learning is not available on most courses.

Timetabling hours

Lectures are timetabled between 9am and 6pm.
Modules cannot be studied that require attending only morning lectures.

Accommodation and childcare

Accommodation is available:

Specifically for mature students	No
For mature students with families	No

The institution does have crèche/childcare facilities.
Number of spaces varies according to site where the student is based.
Spaces are not always available.

General
There are no societies or organised social activities for mature students.
There is no online information specifically for mature students.

University of Wales College Newport
Caerleon Campus
PO Box 179
Newport
NP18 3YG
Phone: 01633 432432
Fax: 01633 432850
Email: uic@newport.ac.uk
Website: www.newport.ac.uk
Total number of students at institution: 8,978
Total number of mature students: 4,525

Student Services Officer
Phone: 01633 432657
Fax: 01633 432063
Email: studentservices@newport.ac.uk

Applications
General entry qualifications that are considered acceptable for mature
applicants without the normal standard entry qualifications:

Access Course	Yes
Essay submission	No
Entrance exam	No
APEL/APL	Yes
Other	Interview

The institution does not interview all mature applicants.

Study
Negotiated flexible learning is not available on most courses.
It is available to:

Full-time students	No
Part-time students	No
Distance Learning students	Yes

Timetabling hours
Lectures are timetabled between 9.00am and 9.00pm.
Modules cannot be studied that require attending only morning lectures.

Accommodation and childcare
Accommodation is available:

Specifically for mature students	No
For mature students with families	No

The institution does have crèche/childcare facilities.
There are 18 spaces (for children aged 18 months to 5 years).
Spaces are not always available.

General
There are no societies or organised social activities for mature students.

University of Wales Institute, Cardiff (UWIC)
Llandaff Campus
Western Avenue
Cardiff
CF5 2SG
Phone: 029 2041 6044
Fax: 029 2041 6286
Email: uwicinfo@uwic.ac.uk
Website: www.uwic.ac.uk
Total number of students at institution: 8,000
Total number of mature students: 1,640 (i.e. 20.5 per cent)

Widening Participation Officer

Phone: 029 2041 6288 or 029 2041 6571

Email: khowells@uwic.ac.uk or swinter@uwic.ac.uk

Applications

General entry qualifications that are considered acceptable for mature applicants without the normal standard entry qualifications:

Access Course	Yes
APEL/APL	Yes

The institution does not interview all mature applicants.

Funding

There are no specific mature student bursaries available over and above the national funds.

Study

Negotiated flexible learning is only available to part-time students.

Timetabling hours

Most lectures take place between 9am and 4pm, but some take place in the early evening.

Modules cannot be studied that require attending only morning lectures.

Accommodation and childcare

Accommodation is available:

Specifically for mature students	No
For mature students with families	No

The institution does have crèche/childcare facilities.

There are 40 spaces.

Spaces are not always available.

General

There are no societies or organised social activities for mature students.

There is online information specifically for mature students at www.uwic.ac.uk/new/widening_participation/mature.asp.

Mature students without standard qualifications are welcome to apply for UWIC courses.

University of Wales Swansea

Singleton Park
Swansea
SSA2 8PP
Phone: 01792 205678
Fax: 01792 295655
Email: admissions@swansea.ac.uk
Website: www.swansea.ac.uk

Student Support Officer

Dawn Hanford
Phone: 01792 295826
Fax: 01792 295157
Email: J.D.Hanford@swansea.ac.uk

Applications

General entry qualifications that are considered acceptable for mature
applicants without the normal standard entry qualifications:

Access Course	Yes
Essay submission	Yes – sometimes
Entrance exam	No
APEL/APL	Yes – sometimes

The institution does not interview all mature applicants.

Funding

There are no specific mature student bursaries available over and above the
national funds.

Study

Negotiated flexible learning is not available on most courses.

Timetabling hours

Lectures are timetabled between 9am and 6pm.
Modules can be studied that require attending only morning lectures.

Accommodation and childcare

Accommodation is available:
Specifically for mature students Yes – University Hall for students over 25.
For mature students with families Yes – there are some family flats.

The institution does have crèche/childcare facilities.

There are 32 spaces.

Spaces are not always available.

General

There are societies or organised social activities for mature students; details are available from the students' union.

There is no online information specifically for mature students.

University of Warwick

Gibbet Hill Road

Coventry

CV4 7AL

Phone: 024 7652 3523

Fax: 024 7646 1606

Email: student.recruitment@warwick.ac.uk

Website: www.warwick.ac.uk

Total number of students at institution: 17,904

Centre for Lifelong Learning

Phone: 024 7652 3683

Fax: 024 7657 4366

Email: lifelonglearning@warwick.ac.uk

Applications

General entry qualifications that are considered acceptable for mature applicants without the normal standard entry qualifications:

Access Course	Yes
Essay submission	No
Entrance exam	No
APEL/APL	Yes
Other	Access to Warwick Degrees – special admissions scheme.

The institution does interview all mature applicants.

Funding

There are no specific mature student bursaries available over and above the national funds.

Study

Negotiated flexible learning is available on most part-time courses.

Timetabling hours

Lectures are timetabled between 9am and 6pm (and some evenings for some part-time degrees).

Some modules can be studied that require attending only morning lectures.

Accommodation and childcare

Accommodation is available:

Specifically for mature students	No
For mature students with families	Yes – for any student with a family, not specifically for mature students.

The institution does have crèche/childcare facilities.

Spaces are not always available, but students' children have priority and there are grants to help with costs.

General

There are societies or organised social activities for mature students. There is a common room for mature students and various ad-hoc activities.

There is online information specifically for mature students on the Centre for Lifelong Learning web pages: www2.warwick.ac.uk/fac/soc/conted.

College of West Anglia

Tennyson Avenue
King's Lynn
Norfolk
PE30 2QW
Phone: 01553 761144
Fax: 01553 815392

Email: enquiries@col-westanglia.ac.uk
Website: www.col-westanglia.ac.uk
Total number of students at institution: 20,000

Student Support Officer

Faye Button
Phone: 01553 761144
Email: fbutton@col-westanglia.ac.uk

Applications

General entry qualifications that are considered acceptable for mature
applicants without the normal standard entry qualifications:

Access Course	Yes
Essay submission	Yes
Entrance exam	Yes
APEL/APL	Yes

The institution does not interview all mature applicants.

Funding

There are specific mature student bursaries available over and above the
national funds.

Study

Negotiated flexible learning is available on most courses.
It is available to:

Full-time students	Yes
Part-time students	Yes
Distance Learning students	Yes

Timetabling hours

Lectures are timetabled between 9am and 9pm.
Modules can be studied that require attending only morning lectures.

Accommodation and childcare

Accommodation is available:

Specifically for mature students	No
For mature students with families	No

The institution does have crèche/childcare facilities.
Spaces are not always available.

General

There are societies or organised social activities for mature students.

University of the West of England

Frenchay Campus
Coldharbour Lane
Bristol
BS16 1QY
Phone: 0117 965 6261
Fax: 0117 328 2810
Email: admissions@uwe.ac.uk
Website: www.uwe.ac.uk
Total number of students at institution: 24,343
Total number of mature students: 12,310

Student Support Officer

Nick Bain
Phone: 0117 328 2555
Fax: 0117 328 2986
Email: student.support@uwe.ac.uk

Applications

General entry qualifications that are considered acceptable for mature
applicants without the normal standard entry qualifications:

Access Course	Yes
Essay submission	Yes
Entrance exam	No
APEL/APL	Yes

The institution does not interview all mature applicants.

Funding

There are no specific mature student bursaries available over and above the
national funds.

Study

Negotiated flexible learning is not available on most courses.

Timetabling hours

Lectures are timetabled between 8.30am and 5.30pm, with some evening lectures until 9pm.

Modules can be studied that require attending only morning lectures.

Accommodation and childcare

Accommodation is available:

Specifically for mature students	No
For mature students with families	No

The institution does have crèche/childcare facilities.

There are 40 spaces (20 for children aged 6 months+ and 20 for children aged 2–5).

Spaces are not always available.

General

There are no societies or organised social activities for mature students at present, but there may be when a Mature Students' Officer is elected.

There is no online information specifically for mature students.

West Nottinghamshire College

Derby Road
Mansfield
Nottinghamshire
NG18 4PJ
Phone: 01623 627191
Fax: 01623 623063
Email: studentservices@westnotts.ac.uk
Website: www.westnotts.ac.uk

Student Support Officer

Phone: 01623 627191
Fax: 01623 429949
Email: ecollins@westnotts.ac.uk

Applications

General entry qualifications that are considered acceptable for mature
applicants without the normal standard entry qualifications:

Access Course	Yes
Essay submission	No
Entrance exam	No
APEL/APL	Yes

The institution does interview all mature applicants.

Funding

There are no specific mature student bursaries available over and above the
national funds.

Study

Negotiated flexible learning is available on most courses.
It is available to:

Full-time students	Yes
Part-time students	Yes
Distance Learning students	Yes

Timetabling hours

Modules can be studied that require attending only morning lectures.

Accommodation and childcare

Accommodation is available:

Specifically for mature students	No
For mature students with families	No

The institution does have crèche/childcare facilities.
There are 35 spaces DR and 20 spaces CR.
Spaces are not always available.

General

There are no societies or organised social activities for mature students.

West Thames College

London Road
Isleworth
Middlesex
TW7 4HS
Phone: 020 8326 2000
Fax: 020 8326 2001
Email: info@west-thames.ac.uk
Website: www.west-thames.ac.uk

Student Support Officer

Amritpal Bansal
Phone: 020 8326 2412
Fax: 020 8326 2001
Email: amritpal.bansal@west-thames.ac.uk

Applications

General entry qualifications that are considered acceptable for mature
applicants without the normal standard entry qualifications:

Access Course	Yes
Essay submission	No
Entrance exam	Yes
APEL/APL	Yes
Other	Initial assessment

The institution does not interview all mature applicants.

Funding

There are specific mature student bursaries available over and above the
national funds.

Study

Negotiated flexible learning is available on some courses.
It is available to:

Full-time students	No
Part-time students	Yes
Distance Learning students	No

Timetabling hours
Lectures are timetabled between 9am and 9.30pm, depending on the type of course.
Modules can be studied that require attending only morning lectures, but this depends entirely on the course.

Accommodation and childcare
Accommodation is available:

Specifically for mature students	No
For mature students with families	No

The institution does have crèche/childcare facilities.
Number of spaces varies.
Spaces are not always available.

General
There is online information specifically for mature students in the 'Adult' section of the main website.

University of Westminster
Central Student Administration
Metford House
115 New Cavendish Street
London
W1W 6UW
Phone: 020 7911 5000
Fax: 020 7911 5858
Email: admissions@wmin.ac.uk
Website: www.wmin.ac.uk
Total number of students at institution: 22,000

Central Student Administration
Phone: 020 7911 5000
Fax: 020 7911 5858
Email: admissions@wmin.ac.uk

Applications
General entry qualifications that are considered acceptable for mature applicants without the normal standard entry qualifications:

Access Course	Yes
Essay submission	Yes
Entrance exam	No
APEL/APL	Yes
Other	Portfolios for architecture/design.

The institution does not interview all mature applicants.

Funding
There are no specific mature student bursaries available over and above the national funds.

Study
Negotiated flexible learning is available on part-time courses.

Other	Some seminar groups are in the evenings.

Timetabling hours
Lectures are timetabled between 9am and 5pm for full-time students (9pm for part-time students).
Modules cannot be studied that require attending only morning lectures.

Accommodation and childcare
Accommodation is available:

Specifically for mature students	No – however, postgraduate accommodation accepts mature students and mature students are usually placed with other mature students.
For mature students with families	No

The institution does have crèche/childcare facilities.

There are 12 spaces at the Harrow Campus, and 20 at the Marylebone Campus.

Spaces are not always available.

Provision is for children over two.

General

There are no societies or organised social activities for mature students. However, there are study skills groups and workshops for mature students. Emphasis is on integration.

There is a handbook available to students before they arrive – this is not specific to mature students but contains useful information, especially financial information.

Weston College

Knightstone Road
Weston-super-Mare
North Somerset
BS23 2AL
Phone: 01934 411411
Fax: 01934 411410
Email: mktg@weston.ac.uk
Website: www.weston.ac.uk
Total number of students at institution: 14,000
Total number of mature students: 600 full-time, 11,000 part-time

Mature Students' Officer

Phone: 01934 411411 ext. 355

Student Support Officer

Phone: 01934 411464
Fax: 01934 411410
Email: bob.hughes@weston.ac.uk

Applications

General entry qualifications that are considered acceptable for mature applicants without the normal standard entry qualifications:

Access Course	Yes
Other	Interview, audition/ portfolio.

The institution does interview all mature applicants.

Funding
There are no specific mature student bursaries available over and above the national funds.

Study
Negotiated flexible learning is available on most courses.
It is available to:

Full-time students	Yes
Part-time students	Yes
Distance Learning students	Yes

Timetabling hours
Lectures are timetabled between 9am and 9pm.
Modules can be studied that require attending only morning lectures.

Accommodation and childcare
Accommodation is available:

Specifically for mature students	No
For mature students with families	No

The institution does have crèche/childcare facilities.
The number of spaces is subject to funding.
Spaces are always available.
The institution uses local childminders, day nurseries and crèches.

General
The students' union organises social activities for mature students.
There is no online information specifically for mature students.

Wimbledon School of Art
Merton Hall Road
London
SW19 3QA
Phone: 020 8408 5000
Fax: 020 8408 5050
Email: info@wimbledon.ac.uk

Website: www.wimbledon.ac.uk
Total number of students at institution: 950
Total number of mature students: 300

Student Support Officer

Kerry Sullivan
Phone: 020 408 5000
Fax: 020 8408 5050
Email: ksullivan@wimbledon.ac.uk

Applications

General entry qualifications that are considered acceptable for mature
applicants without the normal standard entry qualifications:

Access Course	Yes
Essay submission	No
Entrance exam	No
APEL/APL	Yes
Other	Portfolio

The institution does not interview all mature applicants.

Funding

There are no specific mature student bursaries available over and above the
national funds.

Study

Negotiated flexible learning is available on most courses.
It is available to:

Full-time students	Yes
Part-time students	Yes
Distance Learning students	Yes

Timetabling hours

Lectures are timetabled between 9.30am and 4.30pm.
Modules cannot be studied that require attending only morning lectures.

Accommodation and childcare

Accommodation is available:

Specifically for mature students	No
For mature students with families	No

The institution does not have crèche/childcare facilities.

General

There are no societies or organised social activities for mature students. The high proportion of mature students at this institution is evidence of the extent of support available on a one-to-one basis.

Wolfson College

Barton Road
Cambridge CB3 9BB
Phone: 01223 335900
Fax: 01223 335908
Email: ug-admissions@wolfson.cam.ac.uk
Website: www.wolfson.cam.ac.uk
Total number of students at college: 600
Total number of mature students: 600

Admissions Tutor

Phone: 01223 335918
Fax: 01223 335908
Email: tut21@cam.ac.uk

Applications

General entry qualifications that are considered acceptable for mature applicants without the normal standard entry qualifications:

Access Course	Yes
Entrance exam	Required for history, engineering, medicine and English.
APEL/APL	No

The college does not interview all mature applicants.

Funding

There are no specific mature student bursaries available over and above the national funds.

Study

Negotiated flexible learning is not available on most courses.

Timetabling hours

Lectures are timetabled between 9am and 6pm.
Modules can be studied that require attending only morning lectures, but other work is required.

Accommodation and childcare

Accommodation is available:

Specifically for mature students	Yes – 600 rooms.
For mature students with families	Yes – two flats for families.

The college does not have crèche/childcare facilities.
Enquiries about childcare at Cambridge University are dealt with by the childcare office on 01223 332249.

General

There are societies or organised social activities for mature students at the college and at the university as a whole.
There is online information specifically for mature students.
The college does not offer a course in mathematics.

University of Wolverhampton

Wulfruna Street
Wolverhampton
WV1 1SB
Phone: 01902 322222
Fax: 01902 322517
Email: enquiries@wlv.ac.uk
Website: www.wlv.ac.uk
Total number of students at institution: 22,840
Total number of mature students: 14,846

Student Support Officer
Phone: 01902 321020
Fax: 01902 321021
Email: gateway@wlv.ac.uk

Applications
General entry qualifications that are considered acceptable for mature applicants without the normal standard entry qualifications:

Access Course	Yes
Essay submission	Yes
Entrance exam	No
APEL/APL	Yes

The institution does not interview all mature applicants.

Funding
There are no specific mature student bursaries available over and above the national funds.

Study
Negotiated flexible learning is available on most courses.
It is available to:

Full-time students	No
Part-time students	Yes

Timetabling hours
Lectures are timetabled between: 10am and 1pm; 2pm and 5pm; 6pm and 9pm.
Modules can be studied that require attending only morning lectures.

Accommodation and childcare
Accommodation is available:

Specifically for mature students	Yes – on all campuses.
For mature students with families	Yes – on Compton campus.

The institution does have crèche/childcare facilities called Little Scholars Nursery.

There are 50 spaces.

Spaces are not always available.

General

Advice for mature students is available from the Higher Education Shop:

Higher Education Shop
62-68 Lichfield Street
Wolverhampton
WV1 1DJ
Email: heshop@wlv.ac.uk
Phone: 01902 321032

Yeovil College

Mudford Road
Yeovil
Somerset
BA21 4DR
Phone: 01935 845454
Fax: 01935 415483
Email: lynne.stocker@yeovil.ac.uk
Website: www.yeovil.ac.uk

HE Student Support Officer

Phone: 01935 845454
Fax: 01935 415483

Applications

General entry qualifications that are considered acceptable for mature applicants without the normal standard entry qualifications:

Access Course	Yes
Essay submission	Yes
APEL/APL	Yes

The institution does interview all mature applicants.

Funding

There are no specific mature student bursaries available over and above the national funds.

Study

Negotiated flexible learning is not available on most courses.

Timetabling hours

Lectures are timetabled between 9am and 9pm.
Modules cannot be studied that require attending only morning lectures.

Accommodation and childcare

Accommodation is available:

For mature students	Yes – there is a student house with 15 rooms.
For mature students with families	No

The institution does have crèche/childcare facilities.
Spaces are always available.
There is an on-site crèche.

General

The students' union organises social activities for mature students.

York College

Tadcaster Road
York
YO24 1UA
Phone: 01904 770200
Fax: 01904 770499
Email: customerservices@yorkcollege.ac.uk
Website: www.yorkcollege.ac.uk
Total number of students at institution: 13,000
Total number of mature students: 9,000

Student Support Officer

Paul Guilfoyle
Phone: 01904 770200
Fax: 01904 770499

Applications

General entry qualifications that are considered acceptable for mature
applicants without the normal standard entry qualifications:

Access Course	Yes
Essay submission	No
Entrance exam	No
APEL/APL	Yes

The institution does not interview all mature applicants.

Funding

There are no specific mature student bursaries available over and above the national funds.

Study

Negotiated flexible learning is available on most courses.
It is available to:

Full-time students	Yes
Part-time students	Yes
Distance Learning students	Yes

Timetabling hours

Lectures are timetabled between 9am and 9.30pm.
Modules can be studied that require attending only morning lectures.

Accommodation and childcare

Accommodation is available:

Specifically for mature students	Yes
For mature students with families	No

The institution does have crèche/childcare facilities.
There are 35 spaces.
Spaces are not always available.
Community childcare is available.

General

There are no societies or organised social activities for mature students.

University of York

Heslington
York
YO10 5DD
Phone: 01904 430000
Fax: 01904 433538
Email: liason@york.ac.uk
Website: www.york.ac.uk
Total number of students at institution: 9,300
Total number of mature students: 800

Mature Students' Officer

Student Union
Phone: 01904 433724
Fax: 01904 434664

Welfare Information Officer

Denise O'Donnell
Phone: 01904 433730
Fax: 01904 434664
Email: liason@york.ac.uk

Applications

General entry qualifications that are considered acceptable for mature applicants without the normal standard entry qualifications:

Access Course	Yes
Other	A combination of essay submission, entrance exam and APEL/APL. Each applicant is assessed individually.

The institution does interview all mature applicants.

Funding

There are specific mature student bursaries available over and above the national funds.

Study

Negotiated flexible learning is not available on most courses.

Timetabling hours

Lectures are timetabled between 9.00am and 6.15pm.

Some modules can be studied that require attending only morning lectures.

Accommodation and childcare

Accommodation is available:

Specifically for mature students	Yes
For mature students with families	Yes

The institution does have crèche/childcare facilities.

There are 40 spaces.

Spaces are not always available.

These facilities are on campus and are open 5 days a week 48 weeks of the year. There is a reduced fee for student parents. For further childcare information call 01904 433737.

General

There are societies or organised social activities for mature students. There is a Mature Students Association and an Association of University Families. There is online information specifically for mature students at www.york.ac.uk/admissions.

York St John College

Lord Mayor's Walk
York
YO31 7EX
Phone: 01904 624624
Fax: 01904 612512
Website: www.yorksj.ac.uk

Student Support Officer

Phone: 01904 716522

Applications

General entry qualifications that are considered acceptable for mature applicants without the normal standard entry qualifications:

York St John College

Access Course	Yes
Essay submission	Yes
Entrance exam	No
APEL/APL	Yes

The institution does not interview all mature applicants.

Funding

There are no specific mature student bursaries available over and above the national funds.

Study

Negotiated flexible learning is available on most courses.
It is available to:

Full-time students	Yes
Part-time students	Yes
Distance Learning students	No

Timetabling hours

Lectures are timetabled between 9am and 9pm.
Modules cannot be studied that require attending only morning lectures.

Accommodation and childcare

Accommodation is available:

Specifically for mature students	No
For mature students with families	No

The institution does have crèche/childcare facilities.
There are 16 spaces.
Spaces are not always available.

General

There are societies or organised social activities for mature students. These are organised by the students' union mature students' society.
There is online information specifically for mature students.
A college guide for mature students is available.